Coffee Cherry Cocoa Pod
The Coffee Addicts and Chocoholics Handbook

I0422767

Coffee Cherry Cocoa Pod
The Coffee Addicts and Chocoholics Handbook

David Brent

First Printing: 2014
ISBN 978-1500662554

 **COFFEE CONTENTS**

Introduction 1

An Enlightening Timeline Of The Coffee Bean 6

Coffee Brewing In The Ancient World 12

Coffee Brewing In The Modern World 18

Arabica, Robusta, And Liberica 31

The Art Of Roasting- Tan Don't Burn 39

Espresso- The Coffee Lovers Elixir 47

Coffee Bean Characteristics 55

 **CACAO CONTENTS**

Cacao- The Other Bean 62

An Enlightening Timeline Of The Cacao Bean 65

From The Flower Buds To Your Taste Buds 76

Processing Cacao 84

Homemade Chocolate 90

White, Milk, And Dark 94

Holiday Traditions 97

Two Beans 103

Introduction

Time line- 1000 B.C.

Location- Planet Earth.

Just before daybreak. Dawn. Deep in the heart of the Amazon basin there is an oppressive silence. A lingering mist envelops the forest, clinging precariously to the dampness of the new day. Along the riverbank in the dense underbrush a lone seedling stretches down into the fertile loam of the forest floor looking for nourishment. As the first beams of new morning sunlight filter through the rainforest canopy a light rain begins to fall, dissipating the mist and merging with the humidity. Mother earth yawns and embraces the elements. The smell is wet, extremely heavy and overwhelmingly green. New life abounds in the prehistoric forest, waiting to be discovered.

Another day in the evolution of time has begun.

Just before nightfall. Twilight. The air is a lot thinner up here. The evening sunlight slowly fades, relinquishing its hold on the day and slowly yields to the night. The incessant drone of forest insects gradually gives way to the occasional call of a bird or the howl of a monkey. Darkness trickles slowly down the mountain side, stealing away the heat of the day and cooling the night. The temperate rainforest canopy acts like a blanket, insulating the thriving vegetation of the mountainous African landscape. Mother earth exhales and embraces the stillness. The smell is punctuated by newly opened blossoms, reminiscent of jasmine, cloyingly sweet yet crisp and clean. New life abounds in the prehistoric forest, waiting to be discovered.

Another night in the evolution of time has begun.

Timeline- July, 1969.

Location- Outer Space.

The surface of the moon. Four hours before the first moonwalk Houston Control received this message: "Excuse me for a minute. I am going to have a cup of coffee!"

Coffee ... the name alone conjures up images, thoughts, and impressions. A quick brew in the morning on your way to work or school. Long, slow afternoons on the verandah, savoring a rich bowlful. An after-dinner indulgence, enjoyed over your favorite dessert. Coffee has found its way into the lives of millions of people. It is the ultimate aromatic.

Envision being warm and snuggly under the blankets. Something is tugging at your senses. Well, one of your senses. Even though you are three doors down, you can't escape the delightful smell wafting from your kitchen. It's intoxicating. It will make you get out of bed and head to the hub of your home. This is not to say that you will indulge in a freshly brewed cup.

Coffee, as aromatic as it is, is an acquired taste. Some would argue that it is too acidic, or too strong. Many of these doubters, however, have succumbed to the passion of drinking coffee by 'mellowing out' their brew with cream and sugar. Any way you drink it- whether black, light, hot, cold, sweetened, or unsweetened, it's definitely a pleasure. We as human beings are sociable creatures- what better way to socialize than over a perfect cup of coffee? Although specialty coffee drinks are growing in leaps and bounds, they are definitely not 'new.'

Coffee has been around a long time. As legend would have it, sometime between 600- 800 A.D., a young goat herder by the name of Kaldi, who resided in Ethiopia, was tending his goats. He observed them eating the berries of a nearby bush. Shortly thereafter, the goats began to frolic and play merrily. Kaldi, inquisitive goat herder that he was, decided to investigate. He found that, after eating the ripe red berries, he, too, experienced the same stimulating effect.

Neighboring monks soon heard about this remarkable berry. They would dry the berries so they could transport them too far off monasteries. When they arrived at a monastery, they would soak the dried berries in water. They would then eat the berry and drink the caffeine ingested water. In doing this, they believed their senses were more acute during prayer. Soon after, the early Africans started to mix coffee with fat to carry with them when they needed to refuel on their journeys. These were meager beginnings, but the birth of coffee had begun.

Did You Know?

Coffee- the aromatic brew that we all love- actually comes from a fruit...

When the ripe red cherries of the coffee plant obtain a brilliant red hue, they are hand-picked, leaving the green cherries behind. As the green cherries ripen, the plant will be revisited every week to ten days until it is harvested completely.

Some coffee producing countries schedule the school year around the harvest time so that the children can assist in picking the ripe, red cherries. The act of picking only the red cherries is very labor intensive, but it is imperative in producing the world's best coffees.

Inside the cherry are two green coffee beans sitting side by side. Sometimes only one round bean is produced. This is called a peaberry. Some people dispute that the peaberry is a superior bean, due to all of the essence of the coffee being put into one bean, and not into two.

There are two main types of coffee beans produced- Arabica (the very best and hand-picked) grown at elevations of 3000 feet and above, and Robusta, (which contains twice the caffeine) a heartier plant grown at lower altitudes.

The lower the altitude at which coffee is grown, the softer the coffee bean will be. Higher altitudes have less oxygen, resulting in harder coffee beans. When trading coffee, H.B. stands for hard bean, grown at altitudes above 4,500 feet.

A mature coffee plant yields about 5 pounds of green (un-roasted) coffee beans per year which results in less than one pound of coffee beans after roasting. To be more precise, one coffee plant produces roughly only one pound of roasted coffee per year. When you purchase a pound, you have purchased an entire years' worth of one plants growth.

On the average plantation, an acre of coffee trees can produce as much as 10,000 pounds of coffee cherries. This amounts to approximately

2000 pounds of green coffee beans after the cherry has been removed. This in turn translates to about 400 pounds of ready for market roasted coffee beans. The main majority of a plantation owners yearly cost is spent on labor to pay the unsung heroes known as coffee pickers, who are paid per pound of cherry.

After they are picked, the beans are removed from the ripe red cherries, the green coffee beans dried, then graded according to size. If you are purchasing a Colombian coffee for example, Excelso or Supremo are terms referring to the size and not the quality of the bean itself. The same extends to a coffee such as Kenya AA.

Over 53 countries grow coffee commercially and all of them lie within 1000 miles of the equator between the Tropics of Cancer and Capricorn, an area referred to as the bean belt. Millions of bags of green coffee beans are exported from producing countries every year, with Brazil being the largest producer.

The United States imports roughly 1/3 of all coffee exported. Coffee in the United States is only grown in Hawaii and the Commonwealth of Puerto Rico.

In terms of coffee consumption, the U.S. is the leader. Coffee is the third most popular beverage in the world (second only to water and tea), and second only to oil on the world's commodity market.

An Enlightening Timeline

Of The Coffee Bean

Circa 600- 850 A.D.
An Ethiopian goat herder named Kaldi is credited by some for 'discovering' coffee. The early Africans combine coffee with fat, realizing the stimulating result of eating the mixture gives them more energy. The pulp of the cherry is also believed to have been fermented into wine.

1100's- 1300's
The first coffee plants are cultivated by the Arabs. They find that by roasting the beans and boiling them in water they create a brew that is not only stimulating, but enjoyable. Coffee becomes so popular in their culture that it is thrown at the feet of the bride at Arabic weddings as a religious offering. It becomes a staple in Arabic homes, and failing to keep a supply for one's wife was considered *'grounds for divorce.'*

The dried green beans were first roasted in crude clay dishes or in stone vessels over open pit fires. These were the original roasting utensils. Stone mortars and pestles were also fashioned to aid in grinding the roasted beans.

During the rise of Islam, which prohibited the use of alcohol, coffee receives a boost in popularity. It is used as a substitute for wine in spiritual practices where alcohol was forbidden.

Qahwah is the name given to coffee in Arabic, however the term actually means wine. Qahwah, loosely translated in Turkish to the word kahve, and later to the Dutch word koffie, eventually becomes the word we all know as coffee.

Coffee is first served in hand made pottery vessels- this is considered to be the first appearance of a coffee pot.

1400's
The world's first coffee house, Kiva Han, is opened in Constantinople, Turkey.

Due to the popularity of Kiva Han more coffee houses are opened in Constantinople (now Istanbul).The first flavored coffees become widely popular. Spices that are added include anise, cardamom, cinnamon and clove.

Coffee houses continue to flourish and are soon being opened to the south in Mecca, Saudi Arabia. Known as Kaveh Kanes, their popularity grows rapidly. Many local people and traveling pilgrims gather there to drink coffee, socialize and exchange stories.

1500's
In Saudi Arabian Mecca, Governor Khair Beg tries to ban coffee. Not a coffee fan, he is afraid his subject's love of coffee will overthrow his rule. The Sultan believes that coffee is sacred and has Governor Beg executed.

The Arabs carefully protect their monopoly in the trade and marketing of coffee by forbidding it to be taken out of the country. Their efforts, however, are thwarted by the thousands of religious pilgrims who visited Mecca each year. By the end of the 1500's, coffee had already found its way to Turkey, Persia (now Iran), northern Africa and Egypt, making it a lucrative trade item.

In Rome the priests are up in arms. They perceive the stimulating brew a thing of evil which alters the mind. They appeal to Pope Clement VIII to ban this 'devil's drink.' However, Pope Clement, as it turns out, is a coffee fan and baptizes it as a Christian drink. The Pope's blessing opens the door for increased imports of coffee into Italy and all of Europe.

1600's
The Dutch were the first to transport and cultivate coffee commercially, beginning in 1616 with a coffee plant obtained from the Republic of Yemen, on the Arabian Peninsula. By 1658 the Dutch had begun cultivation in Ceylon (an island off the southern tip of India) and at their Indonesian colony on the island of Java.

In 1675, King Charles II of England bans the sale and consumption of coffee, which would in effect close all coffee houses. Knowing that men would gather and discuss politics and current affairs, he felt that he was being plotted against by his subjects. Due to pressure from his own coffee drinking staff, he has a change of heart and reconsiders his proclamation.

It is believed that milk was first added to coffee in Holland, in order to smooth the beverage and reduce acidity.

1700's
The Dutch had established plantations in Malabar, India and in Batavia, on the Indonesian island of Java. Coffee that was grown and exported from the port of Mocha in Yemen was blended with the coffee grown on the island of Java, creating the world's first and most famous blend, Mocha Java. Soon the Dutch colonies had become the main suppliers of coffee to Europe, where coffee had first been brought by Venetian traders in the 1600's.

In Paris, King Louis XIV is presented with a coffee plant from Java, a gift from the mayor of Amsterdam. It is said that sugar was first added to coffee in his court.

A French naval officer, by the name of Gabriel Mathieu de Clieu, who's on leave from his station in Martinique, obtains a cutting from the plant that the mayor of Amsterdam had given to King Louis. He sails back to the island of Martinique and unwittingly populates the entire Caribbean and the New World Americas with coffee.

In Boston, the colonists protest the increased tax on tea by the English Government. After meeting in a local coffeehouse (the Green Dragon) to solidify their plan, they dump tons of tea from an English cargo ship into Boston Harbor. Coffee becomes a staple in American homes and a symbol of patriotism.

In New York City, merchants meet at Tontine Coffee House. They exchange ideas and grow their businesses by trading goods and monies. Meager origins- but the Tontine Coffee House grows into the now famous New York Stock Exchange.

1800's
In London, the coffee houses were busy. As in earlier New York, many business deals were being conducted. A stimulating cup of coffee sharpened the mind. In order to have their cup delivered more quickly, patrons designed a box, labeled 'to ensure promptness.' They would put a pence in the box for the server, so as to obtain their brew more quickly. 'To ensure promptness,' shortened to "tep", is credited as the origin of "tipping."

Lloyds of London, who insure some of the world's costliest goods, was originally a coffee house.

Modernized brewing equipment and coffee bean roasters are at their earliest concepts. The first espresso coffee maker is invented in France. It is discovered that hot air is a good method to roast the green coffee beans to the desired brown hue.

1900's
The first drip coffee maker is invented by Melitta Bentz, a German housewife. She uses a filter made of blotting paper taken from her oldest son's notebook.

In Bremen, German coffee merchant Ludwig Roselius and his assistant Karl Wimmer successfully decaffeinate coffee. The Roselius process involved the use of chemical solvents to extract the caffeine from the beans, today most is done using water.

Instant coffee is invented by a Japanese-American chemist, Satori Kato. An American immigrant chemist from Belgium, George C. Washington, improves the method and mass produces it. Called Red-E-Coffee, it is rationed to U.S. soldiers during World War I. They nickname it a cup of George. (After George C. not the president.)

The secretary of the U.S. navy in 1913 was a man by the name of Josephus Daniels, a teetotaler (not a drop of alcohol for him!). He abolished alcohol on all naval ships, and from that time on the strongest beverage allowed aboard was coffee- soon to be known as a cup of Joe. (And to this day still is.)

After World War I- English soldiers return home. Having had little tea but ample coffee rations at war, they start a revival of coffee in England.

After World War II- Employers realize employees work longer and harder after drinking coffee- this was probably the origin of the now infamous 'coffee break.'

2000's
For coffee drinkers in the United States the city of Seattle has become synonymous with a new type of café culture. From the damp cool climate of the Northwest came a new reverence for brewed coffee, not only dramatically improving the quality of the roasted beans, but the variety of ways it is prepared. This new found enchantment with an old flame has rekindled not only the U.S. but the rest of the world- even countries with great coffee traditions of their own such as Italy, Germany and Scandinavia.

Today it is possible to find gourmet coffee in every major city of the world, from London to Sydney to Tokyo. Although available for hundreds of years, the old adage "there is nothing new under the sun" seems to fall by the wayside as coffee reinvents itself over and over again in the modern age.

Down through the ages man has made discoveries. Not at all complacent, we strive to build on our accomplishments. Coffee is by no means any different. From its lowly origins in the belly of a goat that Kaldi watched over in Ethiopia to a brew made from the excreted droppings of an Indonesian marsupial, the bean has influenced history. We have artfully incorporated four methods of transforming it into a palatable brew, these being- Boiling, Steeping, Filtering, and the addition of Pressure. All of these methods have been incorporated and are still used to brew coffee even today.

Coffee Brewing In

The Ancient World

(Boiling, Steeping, Filtering, and Pressure)

Since the beginning of time when man first discovered fire and fashioned earthen pots from clay, hot water was available for all. Roasted coffee beans were pulverized in a mortar & pestle then added to water and boiled over an open flame. The brew must have been quite bitter as the boiling water would have extracted every nuance of flavor from the ground coffee, even the bad ones. Since the coffee was pulverized to a powder in the mortar, it was fine enough to be swallowed- when the pot was removed from the flame, the mixture was stirred and poured immediately into cups and drank grounds and all. As long as the embers were hot you were in business. An open hearth was a necessity not only for cooking food, but to obtain your daily fix- from roasting your green coffee beans to boiling the water for your fresh brew.

1600's- Boiling Coffee
By the 1600's in East Africa and in Arabia, the people of the desert were so taken with their daily coffee they had taken to heating water in the hot desert sand. They would then combine ground coffee from their packs with the heated water and enjoy a breather from the blazing sun. Hot liquid made you sweat therefore cooled you down. Eventually, the design of the pots would evolve into a new and improved method of brewing coffee.

The Turks of Istanbul were artisans. They worked with many elements among which was copper. It was discovered that copper was a perfect conductor of heat. Combining their love of coffee and their natural talents they fashioned a pot called a cezve. It had a wide base and a narrow top, with an elongated handle to keep your hands away from the open flame. It took boiling coffee to a brand new level. The cezve was soon embraced by other cultures and became commonly known as an ibrik. If you want to brew yourself a more primitive cup of coffee, buy yourself a cezve.

The name cezve (you make the c sound like a j, pronouncing it jez-va) is of Arabic origin, meaning burning log or coal, likely because they were used when heating the pot. The name ibrik is derived from Turkish, meaning pitcher, or long handled ewer. When you use an ibrik, you are brewing traditional Turkish coffee.

Over time, making coffee over a charcoal fire in an ibrik became an art. The Turks refined the boiling process and the brewing of coffee became more of a ritual. The custom of preparing coffee in your home and how it was poured and served to guests became steeped in tradition. Coffee has long been a symbol of hospitality in the Turkish culture. At one time it was such an important part of everyday life that a wife could divorce her husband if he could not provide her with coffee.

Marriage was prearranged in Turkish society. When two families met to discuss a betrothal, the bride to be was expected to prepare the coffee for her guests. This was the only time during the entire proceedings that the bride would be allowed any personal opinion about her feelings on the upcoming marriage. Not allowed to speak however, she delivers her feelings about the matter via the coffee she has prepared. If she is pleased about the wedding the families have proposed, she sweetens the coffee. The sweeter the coffee, the happier she is. If the coffee is served with no sugar at all, her answer is an undeniable no. And there is the occasional bride to be who is so adamantly against the suggested marriage that she salts the coffee instead.

The rituals that are associated with preparing coffee in an ibrik are designed as much to preserve the flavor of the coffee as they are to show respect for those being served. Because boiling coffee for any length of time destroys its flavor and makes it bitter, the process of brewing coffee in an ibrik involves interrupting the boiling process. The water and coffee is brought to just under the boil a total of three times, interrupting the boiling process each time to fill the guest's cups one third of the way.

Brewing with this ancient method requires only five elements- the ibrik itself, water, ground coffee, sugar, and a source of heat.

Brewing with an Ibrik

Any heat source can be used, whether stove top or gas. Gas is the preferred method since the open flame is the closest to an open hearth fire. I prefer a tabletop burner that burns alcohol, so that I can brew at the table with guests.

The most important thing in any type of coffee brewing process is the grind. Turkish coffee must be baby powder fine, as you will be consuming water, grounds, sugar and all. If you follow the next few easy steps, you will be enjoying Turkish coffee in no time.

: Add fresh cold water to the pot. I find that using one of the cups you are going to serve in as a measuring cup works really well- just fill one to the brim and pour it in for as many cups as you are making.

: Add finely ground coffee to the ibrik. I find that a heaping teaspoon per cup works well. Now add sugar to taste- try an even teaspoon per cup and then adjust to your personal preference. This is the perfect time to add any ground spices as well. Try some ground cinnamon, nutmeg or even more traditionally, cardamom. If you grind your own beans, try grinding them with the spices added.

Stir the pot- water, coffee, and sugar (optional spices). This is the only time you will stir. The slurry will form a crust on the top of the water. Put the ibrik onto the (low to medium) heat source. Watch the coffee carefully- when the water just reaches the boil, the resulting steam will cause the protective crust to bubble and create a golden foam. When this occurs, immediately take the pot off of the heat and, going from cup to cup, add a portion of the foam to each one. The foam that forms at first boil is considered the most desirable- everybody shares.

Put the ibrik back on the heat and when the steam comes up under the crust and causes more foam to form around the edge, pour again- 1/3 into each cup. At the third boil, fill all the cups. Serve each coffee with a cup of fresh water to cleanse the palate.

Of course the coffee you use is to your own personal taste. I am particularly fond of using Ethiopian Yirgacheffe- grown in the birthplace of coffee, using the traditional ibrik, conceived in the ancient lands of Arabia.

1700's- Steeping Coffee
Let's just put it this way- the French should be famous for more than their wine (although coffee and wine have many similarities). In the 1700's, they discovered that by simply putting the coffee grounds into a small linen bag and immersing it into freshly boiled water they eliminated those annoying coffee grounds between their teeth. Inadvertently, they brought an end to the ground coffee being boiled at all- and steeped it. The lower temperature was still hot enough to get all the flavor out of the coffee without over extracting it. Viva la France!

1800's- Filtering Coffee
Filtering coffee was already a concept that had been expanded by the French. Leaving the linen bag behind a new device named the biggin had been invented. It consisted of two chambers divided by a

perforated screen. The water and coffee were combined in the top chamber and allowed to filter to the bottom. This concept combined with electrical power resulted in the first coffee percolators and to the first electric drip machine.

A new revolution has begun. In 1881 the streets of the small Surrey town of Godalming in England were illuminated with electric light. Godalming was the first town in the world to have a public electricity supply. Several retailers enjoyed the phenomenon. The power was provided by a water wheel on the local river Wey. This began the local distribution of electrical power that would soon cover the globe.

1800's- Pressurizing Coffee
In 1822, Louis Bernard Rabaut, a resident of France is credited with developing a brewing machine that used pressurized steam to force hot water through the coffee grounds, creating the earliest version of what we now know as an espresso machine. Sixty years later in 1884 the first patented espresso machine was produced by Turin native Angelo Moriondo of Italy. Under the patent it was certified as "new steam machinery". That same year he demonstrated his invention at the Turin General Exhibition. I'm sure coffee lovers lined up and marveled at the speed of his new-fangled coffee machine.

1900's- Pressurizing Coffee
Seventeen years later in 1901, an Italian by the name of Luigi Bezzara was granted a patent of his own for improvements he had made on Moriondo's original machine. Four year after that in 1905 Bezzara's patent was purchased by Desiderio Pavoni who later founded the "La Pavoni" company. La Pavoni is still a big name in commercial espresso machines, and the machines are used by many coffee shop owners.

In 1938, Achilles Gaggia perfected the first espresso pump machine. He applied for and received a patent on the machine- which utilized a pump to produce pressure rather than steam, continuing the evolution of espresso brewing. Today the best machines are pump driven. I'm sure all of the customers enjoying an espresso in his café in Milan were pumped up (!). It took a lot of time and a lot of people to perfect the mechanics of designing a coffee machine that builds up pressure and forces hot water through the ground coffee. Be eternally grateful to the denizens of France and Italy for your shot of espresso.

Coffee Brewing In

The Modern World

There are three key ingredients to making the best cup of coffee at home.

The number one ingredient, in my opinion, is the water. Depending on where you live, the quality of water coming out of your taps can vary greatly. Consider this- 98% of a cup of coffee is water. Taking that fact in hand you can understand its significance. Whether you have a home installed water filtration system, or a manual pour-over filter, utilize it every time you make your favorite brew- you will notice the difference!

Number two on the list? Quality coffee.

: I suggest buying only whole bean Arabica coffee and grinding it yourself. Find a local store or online purveyor who adhere to the same quality guidelines that you do. Coffee begins to deteriorate at the *very moment* it is ground, due to its contact with air.

: Keep whole bean coffee in an air-tight glass container in a cool, dry, dark place. A glass container will not absorb the natural oils contained in coffee. If coffee is kept too long in a container such as plastic, the container will absorb the stale oil and infect the fresh coffee beans added to it.

: Never put whole bean coffee in the freezer. The delicate oils can gel, affecting the taste. Repeated removal can also cause unwanted condensation.

: Although properly stored coffee will keep fresh for up to 30 days, I suggest that you buy only enough for a two-week period. This will assure the optimum freshness.

The third key ingredient? The coffee brewer.

There are many variations available on the market from which to choose. Each is unique in design. Some will require a fine grind of coffee, some a coarser grind. Some will produce a heavier brew, some a lighter brew. I will sincerely ask you to remember this. A cup of quality coffee is only as good as the quality of the equipment used to produce it.

The number one thing to remember about maintaining your brewer is to keep it clean. Coffee beans contain natural oils. It is these oils that heat and expand during roasting- creating the heady aroma and light or dark hue of the roasted coffee bean. The oils can adhere to your brewer and, if not cleaned, can build up over time. The residual oil will become rancid, resulting in a bitter brew.

Now that the basics have been covered, it's time to explore all the different ways to brew the versatile bean. The first step is to take your whole bean coffee and grind it. Each brewer requires its own grind and you can achieve this with the proper grinder. The two most popular types available are the blade grinder and the burr grinder.

The blade type is the most common grinder. It contains a well with a sharp blade in the bottom. Begin by measuring your beans into the well. A good rule of thumb is to start with two tablespoons of coffee beans per cup of water in your brewer and adjust to your personal taste from there. Put the lid on the grinder and press the button. The longer you keep the button down, the finer the grind will be. You will find that timing your length of grind will result in a more consistent outcome. My blade grinder takes 13- 15 seconds to achieve the best grind if I'm using a drip coffee maker.
However, no matter how practical a blade grinder may be, it cannot compare to a burr grinder. Because the blades can only "chop" the beans, you get smaller pieces and larger pieces which result in poorer extraction when the hot water is introduced to the ground coffee. As long as I'm using fresh Arabica beans, my blade grinder is great for an early morning brew, but when I have the time, I always rely on my burr grinder to give me the ultimate cup.

The burr grinder is the second most used in residential homes. It is used in coffee houses to grind their espresso for specialty drinks such as cappuccinos and lattés. The main reason can be defined in one word- which is consistency.The main difference is in its design. It contains a coffee bean chamber which is placed directly above two burr blades. The blades are circular and sit side by side. When the chamber is opened, the coffee beans fall between the rotating blades.The blades can be turned closer together to obtain a fine grind, or farther apart for a coarser grind. You can adjust the blades to your need, whether you're brewing coffee for a crowd, or for a demitasse of espresso after a hard day. For optimum quality and consistency at home, the burr grinder is the way to go.

Remember to keep the coffee bean chamber free of oil- invest in a grinder brush, or even a small paint brush to sweep away any residual coffee grinds that may turn rancid.

The Brewers

Easily the most popular, and undoubtedly on the kitchen counter of almost every home, is the electric drip machine. They got their big push into civilian homes in the 1950's when restaurant owners popularized them. The earliest machines were primitive, however they did their job.They filled the restaurant with a comforting aroma that awakened many a sleepy eyed early morning diner.

Today's modern versions are produced with many options- digital clocks, automatic timers, automatic shut off, permanent gold filters, thermal carafes, to name a few. You can choose from many name brands. Whatever electric drip brewer you choose, to get the optimum performance for the perfect cup, follow these drip tips:

: Brew up to at least 3/4 of your machines cup capacity. Every drip coffee maker contains a heating element. The heating element takes some time to reach its optimum operating temperature. Brewing half a pot does not allow the element to do its job, resulting in a warmer and weaker brew.

: Use cold, fresh, filtered water. Fresh water contains more oxygen, which enhances flavor. Use the correct amount (and correct grind) of fresh coffee.

: Buy a machine with a cone-shaped filter. Due to its shape, it ensures better extraction. When the heated water enters the cone, it is taken from a wide surface to a narrower point, concentrating it. A flat-bottomed filter does not utilize this, thus valuable flavor is lost. The cone shape is also more cost effective, as you will need less ground coffee to get the desired strength.

: Some people argue that a paper filter absorbs some of the coffees natural oils, thus there is flavor loss. Makes sense. If you are a purist, use a permanent gold filter.

: Although tempting, never use your machines stop and pour feature to interrupt the brewing cycle. You are only stealing from the pot and will end up with an inferior brew.

: Always Transfer your freshly brewed coffee into a preheated insulated carafe or thermos. If left on the heat, it will scorch, resulting in a bitter cup.

Also available is a device called the clever dripper. It is simply a filter cone made of glass or plastic which is placed over your cup for a single serving. You measure in the coffee, then pour hot water over the grounds. It uses a #2 paper filter. Most electric drip machines use a #4.....

TIP: To maintain ultimate performance from your electric drip machine, the water lines need to be cleaned periodically. The lines take the water from the reservoir, through the heating element, and finally into the brew basket. Clean lines ensure the optimum heated water temperature required for the perfect cup. When heated water is passed through the line, impurities can build up inhibiting the transfer of heat from the heating element. They can also restrict the flow of the water into the ground coffee. There are commercial cleaners available which will dissolve the impurities, or you can use regular white distilled vinegar. Begin by filling the water reservoir with your choice of cleaner. If using white distilled vinegar, put in three cups. If you are using a commercial cleaner, simply follow the package instructions. Take the brew basket off and place the coffee pot on the warmer. Plug the coffee maker in and turn it on. When the liquid begins to flow through the brew head, turn the coffee maker off. This ensures that the cleaner remains in the lines. After ten minutes, turn the machine on and let some more of the cleaner flow into the carafe. Turn it off again. Two 10 minute intervals will assure that the cleaner has dissolved any impurities in the lines. Now run at least three full pots of water through your machine to ensure you don't get any of the residual cleaner in your brew. Finally, wipe the brew head to remove any oils that may remain. It is a good idea to wipe the brew head regularly after brewing coffee.

Before the electric drip machine became as popular as it is today, people would boil water and pour it into the filter manually. There is still a great brewer on the market today which uses this method- the Chemex.

Timeline- 1936.
Location- United States.

In 1936, a German citizen, by the name of Dr. Peter Schlumbohm, immigrated to the United States. With him he brought a concept for

a new type of coffee brewer. His idea was to use a heavier paper filter that would absorb more of the oils and, perhaps, impurities that a regular pour over would not. The chemist pursued his dream and, in 1941, obtained a patent on his brewer, The Chemex. Due to the heavier, more absorbent paper, the resulting coffee was definitely cleaner, and much brighter, in the cup. His brewer requires a coarser grind.

How does it work?

The glass brewer is hourglass shaped- like two triangles inverted on top of each other. A heavy cone shaped paper filter is inserted directly into the space between the triangles. The thickness of the filter allows water to pass through the coffee grounds in the upper chamber and through into the lower chamber. A regular paper filter would not withstand this pressure and would break.

Brewing with a Chemex

: use a coarser grind of coffee

: boil water and let the kettle stand for 15-30 seconds before pouring. The reason this is important is that water at the boil will actually burn the coffee grounds, resulting in a bitter brew.

: on your first pour, the hot water will push the ground coffee upward, this is called a bloom.

: after the bloom, continue to pour the water in intervals as the coffee slowly filters into the bottom of the brewer.

: it will take some time, and several pour overs. The end result is a considerably less cloudy, cleaner tasting brew.

Some people like to keep their Chemex on a hot plate when entertaining company to keep the coffee warm. I feel it will just scorch and a decorative thermal carafe is the key. Although conceived in the late 1930's the Chemex is still a unique, and eye appealing brewer.

On the opposite end of this spectrum comes a brewer which strives to go in a completely opposite direction. Its name? The Bodum, sometimes called the French press, or cafetiere.

Time line- 1958.
Location- Copenhagen, Denmark.

The earliest glass vacuum pots were created in the early 1800's in Germany. In 1958 Peter Bodum introduces his version- the Bodum Santos. Not only does it have a great appearance, it makes good coffee. Due to the length of time the water is in contact with the ground coffee, you achieve a heavier, more complex cup. His version, which you can still purchase today works like this:

Brewing with a Vacuum Pot

The coffee maker consists of a bottom glass carafe and a top glass bowl that is affixed with a siphoning tube. Cold water is poured into the bottom glass carafe and the top glass bowl is put on top sealing the two. The siphoning tube reaches almost to the bottom of the carafe.

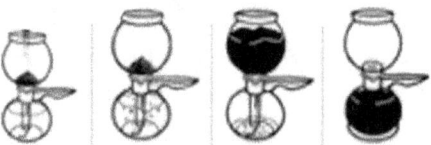

A medium grind coffee is added to the top glass bowl and the unit is put over a heat source, soon causing a vacuum. The vacuum forces the heated water up the tube into the ground coffee. When most of the water has moved to the top bowl, the heat is reduced and the mixture is allowed too steep for a minute or so then taken off the heat. As the bottom carafe cools, the brewed coffee is vacuumed back down the tube. The siphoning tube contains a filter which separates the coffee grounds. This brewer is definitely a conversation piece. If you purchase one–be careful! It is delicate.

In 1974, Peter's son, Joergen Bodum, introduces the first 'Press Pot', also known as a French press, or cafetiere. Everyone has their favorite method of brewing coffee- this is mine.

Again, as with his father's vacuum pot, the Press Pot (or French Press) is designed for more extraction due to the length of time the ground coffee and hot water stay in contact. You will be extracting all of the coffee's essence, oils, and, yes, some sediment.

Brewing with a Bodum (press pot, cafetiere)

Medium-coarsely ground coffee is put directly into the bottom of the glass beaker. Use a tablespoon for every cup size of your Bodum.

Boil water and let it stand for 15- 30 seconds before pouring. Pour the water directly over the grounds, filling to within one inch of the top of the beaker. Stir the coffee / hot water mixture with a plastic utensil (so as to not break the tempered glass) then let it steep for 3- 5 minutes.

There is a reusable filter screen attached to the Bodum's lid. Insert the filter and lid into the top of the Bodum. Now firmly and slowly 'press' the filter to the bottom. The coffee grounds are forced to the bottom, leaving your fresh brew on top. The result, again, is heavy, thick and somewhat grainy, definitely coffee!

TIP: If you are enjoying coffee with someone who enjoys a less intense brew, press the filter ½ way after ½ the steeping time and pour their cup. The coffee's natural oils adhere to the screen's reusable filter, ensuring your heavier brew will remain in the bottom of the Bodum to keep extracting.

After use, thoroughly rinse both the Bodum's carafe and filter screen. Take the screen apart periodically and clean it. Replacement screens, and replacement beakers for that matter, are available.

Now for something completely different! A coffee brewer that implements cold water. Cold water ensures a cup that is very low in acidity- perfect for anyone with a delicate stomach. The great thing about the coffee that this brewer produces is its versatility.

Time line- Early 1960's.
Location- Guatemala.

An American garden nursery owner is in Central America looking to expand his inventory. Taking a break for a cup of Joe, he is presented with a pot of hot water and a carafe of what he finds out is a cold water coffee concentrate. Upon combining the concentrate and hot water, he is amazed at how smooth and mellow the resulting brew is. His name- Todd Simpson. Todd's wife has a delicate stomach. Todd decides to pursue a brew his wife can consume- the result, named after him- the

Toddy Maker. The cold water coffee maker that Simpson devised is incredibly ingenious yet simplistic, consisting of only four working elements- a plastic brewing container, a glass decanter, a thick reusable filter, and a rubber stopper.

How does it work?

Begin by filling the durable plastic container (which is equipped with a reusable filter in the bottom), with one pound of coarsely (percolator) ground coffee. On the bottom of the container is an outlet to place a rubber cork to keep the water in.

Now pour cold water directly over the coffee grounds, filling to the very top of the plastic container. There is no need to stir. Let the cold water and ground coffee slurry sit and steep at room temperature for a minimum of 12 hours, (just leaving it overnight works for me)... then place the container over the accompanying glass carafe, and pull the cork!

The coffee concentrate slowly filters into the carafe. Flavored coffees work great, however when ground, coated beans (such as chocolate or cinnamon) tend to adhere to the filter and take longer to drain.

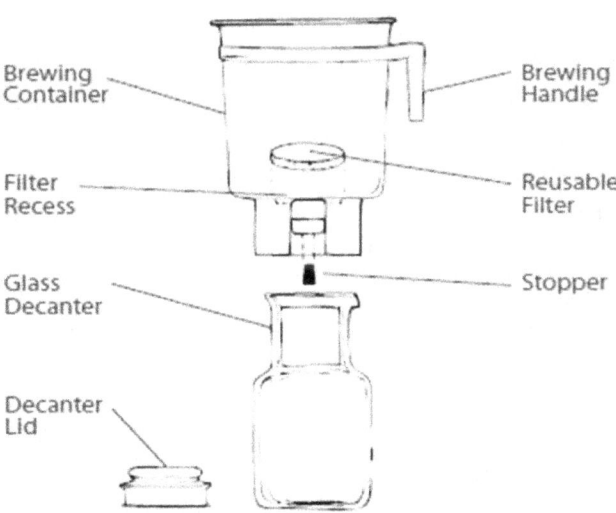

Brewing Container

Filter Recess

Glass Decanter

Decanter Lid

Brewing Handle

Reusable Filter

Stopper

Kudos: The concentrate is definitely less acidic and very mellow. In fact, it is up to 67% less acidic than regular brewed coffee. It can be used to make hot or cold coffee beverages. One-third concentrate combined with 2/3 cold milk sweetened to taste makes an extraordinary iced coffee. I'm talking café quality. Try buying a pound of your favorite flavored coffee to start. Just be sure it is coarsely ground. Then experiment with your own custom blends. A blend of 1/2 cinnamon and 1/2 amaretto is a winner. Using a ratio of 1/3 concentrate to 2/3 hot water, make 'instant' coffee that's not really instant! You can make an awesome iced Café Mocha by using a dark roasted coffee as your base. The concentrate can be stored in your refrigerator for up to a few weeks and can also be frozen.

TIP: A friend of mine who is an avid gardener asked her local coffee shop employees if they would save all of their used coffee grounds for her. She would pick up 6 ten gallon containers of used coffee grounds every week. Her home was only one block away from the shop. One day I went by her house and was awed by her flowers and vast array of plants. It appears that coffee grounds make excellent fertilizer. Use left-over Toddy grounds to fertilize your house plants or garden. You will notice a remarkable difference.

In my mind there is no single correct way to make a cup of coffee. You alone are the best judge of your taste buds. I am amazed at all of the ingenious ways the coffee bean can be used. Earlier I spoke of the four methods of brewing...boiling, filtering, steeping, and the use of pressure. I demonstrated the ibrik (boiling), the drip- both electric and pour over (filtering), and the vacuum pot (pressure and steeping). Notice how both the French Press and the Toddy maker also utilize several methods. Each one uses water to steep and then filter, however one uses hot water, the other cold. They both use reusable filters- one uses a mesh screen filter, the other made of felt. How awesome is the versatility of the coffee bean?

It was predestined to happen…

From that very first fateful sip, I knew it was going to be a lifetime love affair. When I was a boy, my parents would keep their leftover coffee in a container in the refrigerator. Whenever my sisters and I craved a sweet treat, we would combine the coffee with a lot of cream and a lot (!) of sugar. When I was a baby, my Dads mother- my Nana (born in Belfast, Ireland, wouldn't enter a church without a hat and gloves- heaven forbid if a lady ever wore trousers) would give me a tablespoon of half coffee and half milk. She created in me a passion that lives to this day. Long gone, however are my days of milk and sugar. When I reach for a cup of Joe these days, I might as well be eating the beans right out of the bag- strong and black.

Black coffee, in its purest form, contains many cup characteristics. It has many tones and nuances. Brew a pot. Pour a cup. Let it sit for a while, just to cool down a little. Take a sip. Swirl it in your mouth, just to aerate it. Concentrate on what are the higher and lower notes. There is a term they use in the coffee industry that they call 'mouth feel'. It describes the feeling on your tongue. Some coffees 'feel' heavy. Some coffees 'feel' light. Two words that describe coffee are body and acidity. The body is the heavy feel on your tongue. Acidity is the higher note in your cup- not a bad thing! Envision milk and orange juice. Milk, which is heavy, represents the body. Orange juice, with its bright edge, represents the acidity. Do you get the idea? Every coffee producing country yields its own cup characteristics.

Many African coffees are reputed to have a winey taste. Indonesians are famous for their deep, complex, earthy tones. South American coffees are said to be brighter in the cup due to their acidity. For fans of a milder, well balanced cup, Jamaica (Blue Mountain) and Hawaii (Kona) produce awesome coffees. Coffee is like wine. Every country, every region, produces its own unique brew. Many variables factor into the end product- from elevation, to rainfall, to sunlight, to shade, to volcanic soil. Very labor intensive- but well worth the effort.

Coffee is grown and harvested worldwide, however its meager beginnings were in the mountains of Ethiopia in Northern Africa where the tale of Kaldi and his goats began, traced back to as early as the 9th century. By the 15th century, the bean had made its way from Ethiopia across the Arabian Sea to Yemen, on the Arabian Peninsula. The Arabs saw the growing popularity of the bitter brew and began to market the beans. In the next one hundred years it had spread to Egypt, Syria, Turkey, and Persia (Iran). The following one hundred years saw all of Europe becoming enthralled, leading to a glut of coffee houses. Up until the 17th century the Arabs continued to control the market, however like all good things it came to an end. The Dutch secured some seedlings and were successful in germinating them on the island of Java in Indonesia. Mountainous and bounded by the Indian and the Pacific oceans, the conditions were ideal for coffee production.

Coffee plants were now being cultivated in both Africa and Asia and on the Asian islands of Java, Sumatra and Celebes. All that remained was the journey from Asia to the New World- the Americas.

In the mid 1700's a ship sailed out of port to her destination in the Caribbean- a French colony where sugar plantations that manufactured molasses abounded. On board was precious cargo- a cutting from a coffee plant that was a gift from the Dutch to the King of France. The plant was from the island of Java, however its ancestors were from earliest Ethiopia, the birthplace of coffee.

From Paris the ship sailed to the island of Martinique. On the island not only did sugar cane thrive, the coffee plant did as well. The island was in the perfect location to send out ships to Central and South America. The single coffee plant from Java used to populate Martinique was the mother plant to all of the coffee cultivated in the entire Caribbean and the Americas. In fact, all of the coffee plants from the continents of Africa, Asia, and South America, to the islands of the Pacific and the Caribbean, can trace their origins back to the highlands of Ethiopia.

Arabica, Robusta, And Liberica

The coffee plant can conceivably be referred to as a tree because of its vertical trunk and branches. Being in the evergreen family, it keeps its leaves yearlong. The initial shrub can grow to heights of over fifteen feet however on commercial plantations it is kept to about 6 feet or so for the ease of harvesting. Protected from direct sunlight, young plants which are raised in nurseries are carefully planted at the beginning of the rainy season.

The plant begins to flower at three to four years of age but production of the beans takes place only after five. When at their peak the white blossoms are produced in clusters, each of which contain 5 or 6 petals. When it is in bloom, the coffee tree is covered with up to 30,000 blossoms which begin to develop into fruit after 24 to 36 hours. The shape and scent of the petals when blooming is similar to jasmine, giving cause for the evergreen to be referred to as "Arabian Jasmine" in the 17th century.

After only a few days of flowering, the petals fall away and the small green coffee cherries (drupes) appear. They begin to ripen, slowly progressing from green to yellow to a purplish red. The ripening process takes from six to nine months, according to the variety of plant, the altitude it's grown at, and the climate. Depending on the genus of the plant it can produce from one to three pounds of green beans a year.

Growing and caring for quality coffee is no easy feat. Coffee farmers have to be a hearty breed with a good deal of patience thrown into the mix. Consider that from planting the seedling until the first harvest it can take five years. In those five years, the farmer has to contend with fertilizing, watering, pruning, and protecting the plants from the elements. Perseverance and patience. Oh, and it doesn't hurt to be part mountain goat either! The main factors that contribute to quality coffee are soil, elevation, climate & rainfall, and sunlight & shade.

Soil

Coffee requires nutrient rich soil. The best is of volcanic origin, rich in nitrogen, calcium and magnesium. Volcanic soil is fertile and loamy. The coffee plantation also requires good water drainage. The best soil is fertilized by natural leaf litter-fall and from the coffee plants themselves through regular pruning (organic matter). Plantations that utilize shade grown plants (coffee grown under local varieties of trees such as banana) experience less soil erosion. The shade reduces moisture loss and maintains higher temperatures at night.

Elevation

You can safely say that geography has a definite impact on your morning cup of coffee. Coffee can be grown anywhere from sea level to five thousand feet or more. As the altitude it is grown at increases, the longer it takes for the beans to mature. Therefore the beans are harder. This is due to the fact that the temperature is so much cooler and there is less oxygen. Due to the length of time from bloom to mature bean, the flavor profile is enhanced dramatically. High grown coffees are superior. Coffees grown at lower levels have to endure more of the elements. Heat and rainfall cause the beans to mature much more quickly and produce more fruit. Due to this fact, plants grown at lower elevations are a much heartier breed. They produce a higher yield, however the flavor value decreases.

Climate & Rainfall

Coffee is a tropical plant and is only grown between the Tropics of Cancer and Capricorn, an area referred to as the bean belt. This ensures moderate warm temperatures year round. Even the slightest frost can kill a whole crop. The ideal climatic conditions to grow coffee are directly related to air temperature and rainfall. At higher

elevations below the frost-line, the mean yearly temperature should be between 60-70 degrees F. Lower elevations usually average in the range of 70-82 degrees F, with rainfall averaging 60-80 inches per year. If there is less rainfall, man-made irrigation may be required.

Sunlight and Shade

There was a time when the coffee tree grew wild- shaded from the sun under the protection of a canopy of trees. Many organic plantations still grow their coffees this way today. The filtering effect of the shade trees protects their leaves, while they are nourished by the mulch made up of falling leaves. The canopy also aids the rich soil in retaining its moisture.

If you see coffee advertised as bird friendly or songbird, it was grown under shade trees, a natural bird habitat. All young plants are weaned under shade. Mature coffees plants that are grown in full sunlight require more man made fertilizers.

Coffees grown at lower altitudes or on flatter terrain are exposed to more direct sunlight which causes the cherries to mature much more quickly. The plants require more fertilizer, insecticides, and fungicides. This is to ensure the plants are not attacked by leaf rust or insects known as berry borers. The farmer growing at lower levels is also prone to higher soil erosion. High quality Arabica is grown mostly on shade farms, while sturdier Robusta is grown on sun farms.

When referring to Arabica and Robusta in the coffee world, we are talking in terms of economic impact on the world market and quality in the finished cup. Although there are over sixty different varieties of coffee plants, they all belong to the gender Coffea. The two main players are Coffea Arabica (Arabica) and Coffea Canephora (Robusta). Another less known strain with no economic impact at all is Coffea Liberica (Liberica). Plantation owners' worldwide and whole countries for that matter struggle to maintain their presence in the coffee arena so that we, the consumer will enjoy the success of their endeavors. In the end we all benefit. These are the differences in the beans you buy.

Coffea Arabica
(Arabica-from Ethiopia, known from prehistoric times).

Arabica coffee accounts for more than seventy percent of the worlds production. The Arabica plant is fragile and more susceptible to disease. Grown at the highest altitudes of 3,000 to 6,500 feet where the slower growing process concentrates their flavors, they produce a bean that is denser and harder than its counterparts containing roughly half the caffeine.

Arabicas are the only plants that are self-pollinating (they self-reproduce).The cherries will drop from the plant when ripe, and since the cherries ripen at different times, they must be handpicked (selected). The majority of gourmet coffee beans available for purchase are high quality hand selected Arabicas.

: Arabica beans are flatter, longer and their central groove is wavy. They vary in color from light to dark green with a bluish nuance.

: Robusta beans are rounder, more curved and their central groove is straight. They are pale green in color, with brown or grey tones.

Coffea Canephora
(Robusta- from Congo, discovered in 1898).

Grown at the lowest elevations, Robusta is a much more durable plant hence the name. It is derived from a very robust shrub. Containing twice the caffeine as an Arabica, the coffee bean is larger and softer. The plant requires cross-pollination. The shrub itself is more disease resistant and produces a larger crop. Rather than being selected by hand, they are at times strip picked. This is to say the entire plant is stripped of all of its cherries no matter what the ripeness. Robusta coffee is most commonly used in blends (such as espresso), for instant coffees, or can be found in a can at your local grocery store.

Coffea Liberica
(**Liberica**- from West Africa)

Liberica coffee was discovered in the mid 1800's in Liberia, West Africa. It is similar in taste and quality to Robusta. It was introduced to the islands of Indonesia at the end of the 19th century when their Arabica plants were decimated by coffee rust disease. Rust disease affects the leaves of the coffee plant. Less than one percent of Liberica coffee is traded, effectively obliterating it from the world market.

Processing Coffee Cherries
So it's not Ripe, what's the Hype?

As an homage to the superior Arabica bean, I salute the growers who harvest the cherries by only hand selecting the mature red fruit. Coffee, unlike most fruits- will not ripen after being picked. Cherries on the very same branch can be in varying stages of ripeness and be of many different colors. For this reason one plant may have to be revisited in stages over the course of a few weeks. A good picker can gather approximately 100 to 200 pounds of ripe cherries a day. This will yield from 20 to 40 pounds of green coffee beans. At the end of his or her shift, the bounty is carefully weighed and the picker is paid according to the fruits (!) of their labor. It's super labor intensive. All of the beans from the days take are combined and are now ready for processing.

Processing coffee begins in two specific ways, one being the wet process and the other the dry process. To fully understand both, we need to know a little bit about the composition of the coffee fruit itself. The skin is the outermost layer. It is similar to that of a grape, but it's a lot more leathery. Next is the pulp. Think of a grape again, with a similar texture. Part of the pulps makeup is a thick and sweet viscous substance known as the mucilage. Next comes the parchment, a thick paper-like layer which is actually the hull of the fruit. Another thin layer called the silver-skin protects the actual bean itself.

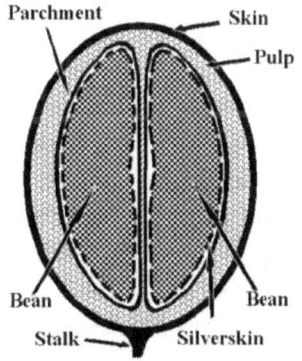

35

When talking about the wet and dry methods of processing the beans, we are actually referring to the removal of all of the protective layers (skin, pulp, and parchment), exposing the bean itself.

The Wet Process

The wet process involves removing both the skin and pulp before the beans are dried. When the beans arrive at the processing plant, they are immediately immersed in a large tank of water. The dense, healthy cherries sink to the bottom of the tank, leaving the lighter weight floaters behind. The healthy, heavier cherries are then pressed against a perforated screen, pushing the slippery beans through to the other side. The skin and most of the pulp (and mucilage) is left behind. The green beans now enjoy a 12 to 48 hour bath in fresh water to ferment.

Fermentation removes any remaining mucilage from the parchment. The process occurs naturally, caused by enzymes that are already present in the beans themselves. After the fermentation is complete and all of the mucilage has been removed the beans are thoroughly washed and are no longer sticky. They are now ready to dry.

Still encased inside the parchment and silver-skin, they are dried in the sun where they need to be raked every 6 hours to promote even drying. A moisture level of 12 to 13 percent is the desired goal. The beans sometimes finish their drying process by machine where they reach an optimum moisture level of about 10 percent.

The Dry Process

The dry process is an age old method of processing coffee beans. It is done only in countries that have a hot and dry climate. The ripe cherries are picked from the tree and simply laid out to dry in the sun on a large concrete patio. As the cherries dry, they must be raked so as to prevent mildew from forming. The process can take from two to three weeks to accomplish. When they are dried, the skin, pulp and parchment are removed. In this day and age the removal (hulling) is done mechanically. Dry processed coffee is known as "unwashed" or "natural". Yemen, Ethiopia, and Brazil produce most of the world's dry processed coffees.

The Semi Dry Process

The semi dry process is a less known and lesser used way to process coffee. Similar to the wet method, the beans are immersed in water, pulped (the skin is removed) and they are immediately dried without fermentation. This method is practiced mostly in Indonesia and sometimes in Brazil.

Processing coffee is part of the journey that takes the freshly picked cherry from the branch to the bag. Like any journey in life, it begins with one step. The first step is hand selecting the fruit. Next, it's on to the removal of the skin and pulp. Then the beans, still encased in their protective layer of parchment, are dried. Now it's time to take the final steps from harvesting to export. These include hulling, sorting and grading.

Hulling

Hulling is the act of removing the parchment (hull) from the bean. In earlier times, the parchment had to be rubbed off of the dry green coffee bean by hand. Nowadays it is mostly done by machine.

Grading and Sorting

Before they are ready for export, the beans are precisely sorted by size and weight. The reason for this is twofold- firstly the grade (size of bean) comes into play when describing a coffee- for example, Kenya AA, 'double A' being the grade or size of the bean. Secondly it is imperative that the beans be of uniform size when roasting to ensure an even roast. Grading is achieved by passing the beans through a series of different sized vibrating screens. They will also be sorted, that is to say closely evaluated for color flaws or other imperfections. Coffee beans that are discolored or flawed will be eliminated.

Finally, after planting, growing, harvesting, and processing, we can safely say it's in the bag. Literally. From this point on the processed dry beans are referred to as green coffee. They are packed into individual bags called jutes (each bag weighs roughly130 pounds and contains roughly 600,000 coffee beans!) or in bulk inside of large plastic lined crates. From there the green coffee is loaded into the hold of a cargo ship bound for the importing country. Millions of pounds of green coffee is exported from producing countries every year to large commercial companies as well as entrepreneurial artisan self-roasters. (Look for one in your neighborhood!)

The Art Of Roasting

Tan Don't Burn

Tan, don't burn. Advice well taken when you go to the beach. Hopefully carrying a nice big cooler of iced coffee. But I'm not talking about the heat from the sun here. I am in fact referring to the act of enveloping the green coffee beans in a super-heated environment for a controlled period of time, also known as roasting. Like a seasoned chef closely watches his meal so it won't burn, so the roaster tends to his beans. Each bean requires a different roast level to maximize its flavor profile. So I repeat- tan your beans, don't burn them.

When you roast a coffee bean, you are in effect altering its chemistry. This chemical altering process is known as pyrolysis. Flavor components that are trapped in the bean are altered and enhanced. Coffee beans contain natural oils which include sugar and starch. During the roasting process, these oils, (or caffeol), caramelize and begin to come to the surface. The longer you roast the bean, the more oil is released and the darker the bean becomes. Interestingly enough, the caffeine contained in coffee escapes along with the oil- therefore dark roasted beans have less caffeine.

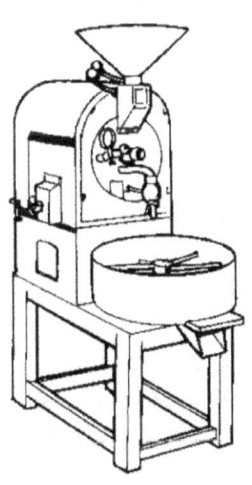

A roaster is similar to a clothes dryer in that it blows dry heat into a rotating drum. As the green coffee beans are tumbled and heated, they go from a green to a yellowish color and finally to a light brown (and sometimes) black color.

A typical roast takes between 9 and 13 minutes at temperatures between 400° and 480°F. As the beans roast, they release an aroma that is similar to that of toasted bread or popcorn. When popcorn pops, it is due to the moisture that is contained in the kernel expanding and breaking through the hard shell- this is not unlike a well roasted coffee bean.

First Crack
The green beans are added to the roaster and the roasting process begins. As the beans get hotter and hotter, they begin to lose weight and double in size. As they succumb to the heat and loss of moisture a loud pop or cracking noise occurs. This is due to the moisture that remains bursting out of the coffee beans. At this point, the sugars contained in the natural oils have caramelized, and the coffee has reached a level known as light roast.

After the first crack, the light roasted coffee beans continue to caramelize and release oils. During this phase, the coffee roasts very quickly. The color of the bean darkens rapidly and a skilled eye and perfect timing are required to achieve the desired roast level. Having reached a darker roast level, the roasting process is usually stopped sometime during this phase.

Second Crack
If allowed to continue roasting, another crack will be heard, although sometimes it is inaudible. If the second crack is desired to obtain an even darker roast, great care is needed as all of the sugars in the coffee will have caramelized, and over roasted coffee can produce a very harsh, bitter cup.

Stopping the Roast
The art of roasting in itself is very sensory. It requires hearing as well as sight and smell. The artisan roaster uses the aroma and color of the coffee to determine when the coffee is done roasting. It takes a great deal of knowledge and experience to know exactly when to stop the roasting process. In order to ensure that the beans stop roasting immediately, the roasted coffee must be cooled quickly. Cooling is usually performed by flooding the roaster with fresh cold air.

Coffee purveyors and roasters have attached many names and definitions to their favorite roasts, and there is no standard term to which they must adhere. With so many different roasts available to choose from, it can get a little confusing. Your taste buds should rule your decision. Generally speaking though, there are four categories of coffee roasts, these being Light roast, Medium roast, Medium-dark roast, and Dark roast. Within these four color categories, you will find some the most frequently named roasts listed below.

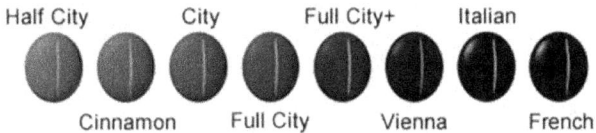

Light Roasts

Light brown in color and light bodied, this roast is generally preferred for milder coffee varieties. A light roast gives a very subtle more delicate flavor. They have a non-oily surface, because they are not roasted long enough for the oils to break through.

Light City, Cinnamon, Half City, and New England Roast.

Medium Roasts

Medium brown in color with a stronger flavor and more body, and a non-oily surface. This roast is often referred to as American roast because it is generally preferred in the United States.

Breakfast Roast
 - a bit sweeter and stronger than a light roast.
American Roast
- well balanced, nice body and acidity, good aroma.
City Roast
- a little darker than the standard American roast.

Medium-Dark Roasts

Rich, dark color with some oil (a sheen) on the surface and with a slight bittersweet aftertaste.

Full City Roast
- which is even darker than City roast.

French Roast
- also known as Dark Roast. French Roast beans brew a dark heavy cup.

Continental Roast
- which is slightly lighter than French Roast but with spicy body.

Viennese Roast
- which is roasted a little longer than regular American roast and has rich chocolaty body.

Dark Roasts

Shiny black beans with an oily surface and a smoky well roasted taste. Dark roast coffees range from slightly dark to almost burnt and the names are often used interchangeably.

New Orleans, European, Italian, and Espresso Roast.

Whatever brewing method you use, dark roast coffees lend themselves easily to an after dinner get together. A steaming bowlful of a dark roasted Arabica coffee served with a super sweet dessert such as baklava is like heaven to me. Dark roast coffee and anything at all sweet are the perfect pair.

All of us enjoy dropping by a cafe for a freshly prepared gourmet coffee to take a break from our hectic lives. Letting somebody else take care of you is one of life's simple pleasures. However when it comes to taking care of guests in your own home, or just treating yourself, there is nothing more satisfying than preparing your own specialty coffee drinks. An after dinner espresso is highly recommended by my way of thinking.

If you want the perfect introduction to brewing straight espresso at home, the Moka pot is a great way to start. It is the closest you will get to a true demitasse of espresso coffee without investing in an electric espresso maker. The brew that it produces not as clean as a traditional espresso, however it

has many of the same cup characteristics.

In 1918, Alfonso Bialetti returned to his native Italy from France (where he had been working in the aluminum industry) to start a small workshop manufacturing household goods. During the 1920s while enjoying an espresso in a local café, he envisioned being able to make the same coffee at home. Taking the initial principal for his invention from a clothes washing machine which drew heated water up from the bottom of a boiler and redistributed it over the clothes, he got to work. At the time, an embargo had been imposed by Mussolini's government on stainless steel. Bialetti had worked with aluminum previously, and as Italy had a rich source of aluminum ore, there was an ample supply. So ample, in fact, that aluminum became known as the 'National Metal' of Italy.

In 1933 the first Moka pot became available to the public. The distinctive design and octagonal shape was based on a silver coffee service which was popular at the time in wealthy Italian homes. The design (and the aluminum construction) has stayed exactly the same as when it was invented. Bialetti's stove top espresso maker is also known as a machinetta (little machine). Aluminum is still used when making the Moka pot to this very day, as it is claimed that the residue of previously brewed coffee that stains the inside of the upper chamber pot adds flavor and depth to future brews.

The machinetta can be likened to an espresso machine in that it brews under pressure, extracting much more of the coffees natural oils. The resulting brew shares some similarities with a conventional espresso machine as well- with the right blend of coffee and the right grind you can actually obtain some fairly decent crema (a golden foam floating on the surface of your finished brew). The finished coffee tastes very similar to a cup of espresso but is somewhat muddier and much less refined. The biggest difference is that the Moka pot brews under substantially lower pressure- 21 pounds per square inch (compared to an espresso machines 130 psi), and uses a mix of boiling water and steam at above 212°F, rather than the heated water (196–205°F) of an espresso machine.The Moka Pot works best with a dark roasted coffee such as a French or Continental. An even darker Italian or Espresso roast also works well. I find that beans that are lighter roasted become a little too acidic in the final cup due to over extraction.

The pot consists of only three parts- a bottom chamber which holds the water and is equipped with a pressure release valve, a funnel filter which holds the coffee grounds, and the top chamber (which contains a filtering screen) where the brewed coffee ends up. The pots are available in 3, 6, and 9 cup sizes (demitasse).

The Brewing Process

Begin by filling the bottom chamber with fresh water. Fill the chamber only to the bottom of the pressure release valve.

Fill the funnels filter basket with ground coffee and then level it off. There is no need to tamp (compress) the coffee into the filter basket because as the water reaches the ground coffee it will expand- effectively doing the tamping for you. You would tend to think the coffee needs an espresso grind- it doesn't. The grind needs to be a little more course.

Insert the funnel basket into the water chamber, and screw on the top chamber. Screw on firmly to obtain a good seal. (There is a rubber gasket that ensures this).

Place the pot onto the stove top on medium- high heat. With the addition of heat, the water in the bottom chamber boils and expands, forcing it up the funnel into the funnel basket, and through the filtering screen into the top chamber. You will know when the process is done when you hear a distinctive 'gurgle' that signifies the coffee is ready to pour- or simply open the lid and have a look.

TIP: Don't try to make less coffee by under-filling the basket, or to make it stronger by over filling it and tamping it. This will affect the extraction process and will result in either weak or bitter coffee. If you need a different number of cups, you should buy another appropriately sized Moka pot.

Brewing a Cafe Cubano

A bonus- using your Moka pot to brew traditional Café Cubano. Place 4 heaping tbsps. of white sugar into a glass measuring cup. Using a 6 cup pot brew some Cuban coffee (available in vacuum packs in the coffee aisle of your local grocery store).

Keeping the lid open, place the pot on the heat source. When the very first of the brewed coffee enters the top chamber, pour a few tbsp.'s of it into the sugar. Close the lid and put the pot back on the heat to finish brewing. With a spoon, stir the sugar and coffee together. Take out your aggravations- briskly stir until the sugar and coffee are a caramel color- stir until the Moka pot finishes brewing.

When the pot has finished brewing, pour the coffee into the whisked sugar while continually stirring. When the coffee and sugar are thoroughly mixed, let the coffee sit for a minute. You will obtain a nice foam (espuma). While gently swirling the measuring cup, distribute the sweetened coffee and espuma evenly into demitasse cups. Cubano perfection.

TIP: Before using your new machinetta for the first time, wash it in mild soapy water and thoroughly dry it. You may want to initiate your first brew by throwing it away as it will taste of newness. The intent is to season the machine before drinking the coffee for the first time and also to be sure the pressure relief valve is working properly. Don't put the pot in the dishwasher. Keep the filter screen clean, and over time as needed you can buy new rubber gaskets. With the proper care you will be brewing countless demitasse cups of espresso.

Speaking of espresso…

The term espresso, although debated heatedly, is likely derived from the process of applying pressure to the ground coffee- from the Latin word expresere, meaning to press out.

If you are looking for an energy boost, make your espresso shot a double. Coffee beans contain natural oils. During the roasting process, the oils are forced to the bean's surface. Caffeine, which is contained in the natural oil, is also forced out. Consequently the darker the roast is, the less caffeine the bean contains. Espresso roast coffee contains less caffeine than a lighter roasted coffee. Contrary to belief a single shot of espresso contains less caffeine than a standard cup of coffee.

·8 oz. cup of Coffee - 85 milligrams of caffeine
·1 ½ oz. Espresso shot - 65 milligrams of caffeine

Achilles Gaggia perfected the first espresso pump machine in Italy in 1938. The Gaggia machine is a favorite in cafés and can still be found in thousands of homes and coffee houses worldwide.

Three years before Gaggia's accomplishment, another Italian, Alfonso Bialetti, created the first aluminum stove top espresso maker. It was such a hit it is estimated it was in 90% of all Italian homes and made the Guinness Book of World Records.

The term Americano is thought to have come from US soldiers in World War II France. They would dilute their espresso with hot water to obtain a strength more comparable to American taste. The French would scoff- Ahh! Americanos!

Espresso- The Coffee Lovers Elixir

ELIXIR- no other word can suffice! Taken from the early Arabic term 'al-iks-Ir'- it literally means remedy, or cure-all. Can you relate? Only the most indulgent coffee fans can appreciate the purism of the act of partaking in a freshly pulled shot of espresso. It trickles out of the portafilter like honey- filling a demitasse cup with 3/4- 1 ½ ounces of liquid gold topped with a velvety crown of crema. It is meant to be savored. Remember these three words- Savor the moment. Straight espresso reacts quickly to oxygen, and is meant to be consumed immediately after brewing. A moment in time. Coffee lover's nirvana. But I digress…

There is a way to produce your favorite coffee house drinks at home without visiting your local café. If you are going to purchase an espresso machine, spend the extra money and buy a quality machine that is pump driven. You can purchase a less expensive electric espresso machine that works by pressure alone, but the resulting brew will be muddier and much less refined. A pump driven machine develops a lot more pressure, obtaining full extraction of the essential oils and thus flavors that are hidden inside the espresso bean.

'**Pulling**' a shot of espresso.

Fill the espresso machines reservoir with fresh filtered water. The fresh water that is stored in the reservoir is drawn into the machine where it is quickly heated to at least 190° F, and then forced through a portafilter containing finely ground espresso roast coffee.

Begin by filling the portafilter with freshly ground espresso roast coffee. Next, 'tamp' the coffee. The purpose of the tamp is to ensure an even surface for the heated water to flow through. The even surface, combined with the proper grind, ensures ultimate extraction. Place the tamper onto the ground espresso coffee in the porta filter and apply an even pressure. The coffee is compressed into the filter. The

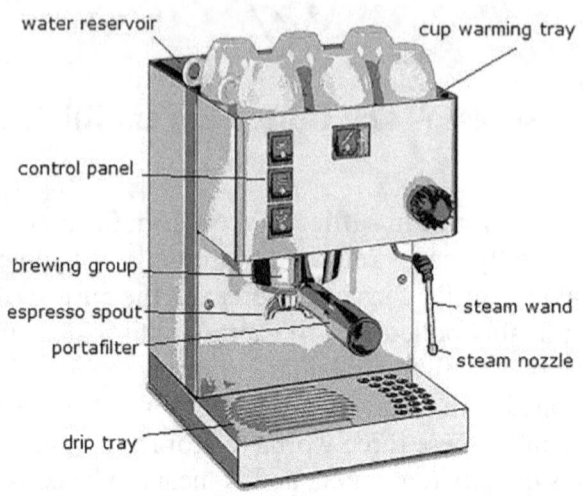

water reservoir

cup warming tray

control panel

brewing group

espresso spout

portafilter

steam wand

steam nozzle

drip tray

grind of the coffee, combined with the tamp, will both be major factors in your shot of espresso. You will find your own personal style of tamp by practice- some do a straight up tamp, some 'polish' the tamp by twisting the tamper on the surface of the coffee in the portafilter. Either way, you want that even surface.

Once tamped, be sure that the rim of the portafilter is free of coffee grounds. Wipe the rims surface with your fingers to ensure this. The reason this is important is that there is a rubber gasket on the brewing group head on the espresso machine which has direct contact with the portafilter's rim- this creates a seal which allows the pressurized hot water to obtain optimal extraction of the ground coffee.

Take the portafilter and, starting on the left hand side of the group head, raise it into place and find where it fits. Now slide the portafilter to the right until it feels firm- don't over tighten. You are now ready to pull a shot of espresso. If everything has been done properly- freshly filtered water, freshly ground espresso roast coffee, the proper grind

48

and tamp- you are golden! Close your eyes and inhale . . . experience the moment. . . but don't wait too long- your precious brew is awaiting! It is the perfect combination of all your efforts- enjoy it!

 Whether you grind your own coffee at home or have your favorite coffee house grind it for you, find the right grind. Invest in a kitchen timer. A perfect shot of espresso should be at 190°- 200° F and will take 17- 24 seconds to pull. The grind and tamp will assure this time line. The espresso will flow slowly, in a honey like consistency. The sign that you have achieved your quest is the crema, a golden foam floating on the top of the brew.

Coffee contains natural oils- some soluble that dissolve in water, some non-soluble, which don't dissolve. The crema is made up of the non-soluble undissolved oils floating on the surface of your brew and makes the perfect espresso shot... perfect! Many espresso blends are made up of Brazilian beans with a small amount of Robusta added to increase body and balance the acidity. It is also believed that the hint of Robusta also produces an increased amount of crema.

There are many ways to utilize espresso, but the three most well-known drinks are the cappuccino, the latté, and the café mocha. They all share two basic components- espresso coffee and steamed milk. The combination of the two is enjoyed by millions of people every day.

Steaming the milk.

Steaming the milk is the major taste factor in all specialty coffee drinks. The act of steaming the milk alters its chemistry, sweetening it. What you will need to create your drinks are some cold milk, a stainless steel steaming pitcher, a kitchen thermometer, and a lot of practice.

TIP: remember this... the colder the milk and the lower the fat content, the better froth you obtain. So- cold skim milk makes the best froth. Here is some great advice- always keep your steaming pitcher in the refrigerator or freezer. You can also cool your milk further before using it by putting it into the freezer for a half hour or so before preparing your drinks.

To froth the milk-

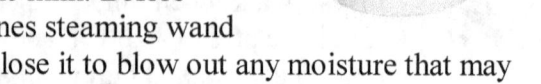

Add the milk to the steaming pitcher until it is just below half full. (The milk will expand.) Place the thermometer in the milk. Before placing the espresso machines steaming wand into the pitcher, open and close it to blow out any moisture that may have accumulated in the line.

Now, place the wand into the milk, just beneath the surface, and slowly open it. The steam will expand and froth the milk. This takes some practice- if the wand is too deep you will have no froth, too close to the surface and you will get large, wet bubbles. I call the right spot for the wand to be the 'happy place.' Listen! You can actually hear the happy place. Continue to steam and froth the milk until it reaches a temperature of 160° F.

Turn off the steam wand and set the pitcher aside for 30 seconds or more. This will allow the milk to condense and give you a more luxuriant froth. It also gives you time to wipe the milk off of the steaming wand and open it to blow out any milk that may have accumulated inside.

To make the three most popular coffee house drinks at home, follow these basic guidelines.

Cappuccino
1/3 brewed espresso, 1/3 steamed milk, and 1/3 frothed milk.   .

Café Latte
1/3 brewed espresso, 2/3 steamed milk with very little or no froth.

Café Mocha
1/3 brewed espresso, 2/3 steamed milk, liquid chocolate (such as Hershey's), whipped cream.

Espresso Lingo

Espresso Shot sizes (traditionally 1.5 ounces).

Single- one shot, Double- two shots,
Triple- three shots, Quad four shots.
Ristretto (restricted) or short.
Doppio (double).
Lungo (long).

Or try an espresso shot....

Con Panna- topped with whipped cream.

Romano- with a twist of lemon added.

Macchiato- 'marked' or topped with a spoonful of frothed milk.
(traditional).

Americano- 1/3 espresso, 2/3 hot water.

Drink Lingo

Shot in the dark (Aka Red eye)- an espresso shot in a regular cup of
coffee.

Tall- Regular Size.

Grandé- Large Size.

Café au Lait- Regular coffee with steamed milk.

Skinny- Made with skim milk.

Brevé- Any specialty espresso-based drink made with half & half
cream instead of regular milk.

Foamless, Naked, Whipless- with no froth or whipped cream.

Harmless- Decaffeinated.

Half Caff- 1/2 Regular, 1/2 Decaffeinated.

Half Caff ? Yikes! O.K. - So you need your coffee decaffeinated.

The two most commonly known methods used to achieve your cup of decaffeinated coffee are the solvent (direct & indirect), and water processes. Green coffee beans are decaffeinated prior to roasting, and must be first soaked with water to make them absorbent.

Decaffeinating Coffee

<u>Solvent Process</u>

- Direct Solvent Process
The beans are first steamed, causing them to swell and become porous. They are then put into direct contact with the solvent for a specified period of time. During this time frame the solvent extracts the caffeine from the beans, which are again steamed in order to remove any remaining solvent.

- Indirect Solvent Process
The beans are soaked in hot water, and the water extracts almost all of the caffeine. Unfortunately it also removes flavor compounds as well. The water is then removed from the beans and mixed with the solvent. The caffeine and solvent are removed from the water and then the decaffeinated water is reintroduced back to the porous beans where they soak up most of the lost flavors.

<u>Water Process</u>

- Swiss Water Process
With a few changes the process is similar to the indirect solvent process. To begin, a batch of green coffee beans are soaked in hot water and then they're discarded. The water solution from the

discarded beans is then filtered through activated charcoal to remove the caffeine but keep the flavor compounds. The flavored water is then introduced to a fresh batch of beans. The idea is that the flavor charged water cannot extract any more flavor (only the caffeine) from the new beans.

- Sparkling Water Process
To begin, the beans are soaked in a pressurized container of purified water, then carbon dioxide (a naturally occurring element) is added, basically creating sparkling water. The carbon dioxide acts as a magnet and extracts the caffeine. The carbon dioxide only affects the caffeine and the flavor molecules remain intact. After decaffeination, the carbon dioxide is recycled and reused.

All of the decaffeination methods used today are closely regulated. The most widely used solvent is ethyl acetate, a natural substance found in many fruits. The water and the carbon filters used are also common elements, as well as carbon dioxide, which is a natural gas that is compressed into liquid form. Any residual components left after decaffeination are miniscule and any that remain at all are basically erased during the brewing process.

Espresso (whether regular or decaffeinated) is not a bean!

Whether you are a seasoned home schooled barista (coffee bartender), or just starting the journey to making perfect espresso based drinks, get the thought of buying espresso beans out of your head. There is no such thing as an espresso bean. Espresso is a term that refers to a roast (roast level). It is a darker roast which in turn produces a darker, oilier bean. For example, you could visit a coffee shop or artisan roaster and purchase a pound of coffee to take home. You might buy a light espresso roast, or a pound of regular espresso roast coffee beans. The roaster simply used the very same beans- from the very same sack of unroasted green coffee beans- and roasted some of them for a shorter or longer period of time.

Another other factor that may also have come into play is whether the roaster used one variety such as a straight Brazilian, or a customized blend of two or more beans. For cxample, a Brazilian Arabica used because of its characteristics of moderate acidity, nuttiness and bittersweet tones, blended with a touch of Vietnamese Robusta to produce a better crema.

Coffee Bean Characteristics

(Why blend?)

In terms of coffee, a characteristic is one facet of a flavor profile. It combines the way a coffee feels in your mouth and the flavor it brings along. For example, one coffee (tasted black) may feel heavy on your tongue (one facet) and have a bittersweet chocolaty taste (a different facet). Another coffee may feel sharper on your tongue and have a winey taste. If you were to combine the two coffees, you would bring the heavy (known as body) chocolaty taste together with the sharper (known as acidity) winey tasting coffee- combining all of these facets would produce a brand new flavor profile.

To evaluate the aroma, flavor, and body of a coffee, roasters and retailers usually conduct a tasting, which is also known as a cupping. What they are trying to do is capture the very essence of the coffee- every nuance available with every human sense available through smell and taste. Before the coffee can be accepted from the seller they must know it is of the quality and standards that they require. A cupping discloses aroma, taste, body and acidity- all of the factors that result in the ultimate final cup.

Cupping

To begin, the green coffee is roasted in small batches and allowed to cool and degas. During roasting, some of the natural sugars in the bean are transformed into carbon dioxide gas. When cooled the beans continue to emit the gas for another 24 hours. After degassing, the coffee is ground and measured into individual cups. The person doing the cupping will smell the freshly ground coffee to get an initial idea of quality. Then water just below the boiling point is added to the cup making sure all the coffee grounds are saturated. The coffee is not stirred. After about 4 minutes, it is time to break the crust. Using a spoon, the taster (cupper) breaks through the coffee crust that has formed at the surface and inhales deeply. The idea is to get your nose as close to the surface as possible and envelop yourself in the aroma.

Next, the floating crust is removed and the tasting begins. Taking a spoonful of liquid, the cupper slurps the coffee heartily and inhales it into their mouth, saturating their tongue and taste buds with coffee as well as air. This allows every nuance of the coffee to be tasted. The coffee is spit out rather than swallowed, although the final taste may involve swallowing to determine aftertaste and how the coffee finishes. Some of the characteristics a cupper may find in a coffee range from sweet to sour or grassy to woody. The coffee might be light or heavy bodied, acidic or smooth. It can be fruity or chocolaty.

Coffee is grown in more than 50 countries and each one is roasted to a specific level in order to enhance its own distinguishing features. Over 70% of coffee that is exported is Arabica, with Vietnam, Brazil and Indonesia contributing the most Robustas.

1) Brazil
Brazil is the largest coffee producing country exporting about one third of all the coffee produced in the world. They have maintained this top position for around 150 years. They produce both Arabica (about 80%) and Robusta beans. Brazilians have always been a favorite for blending. Beans of merit- Bourbon Santos, Mundo Novo, Caturra.

2) Vietnam
Vietnam is the world leader in the production of Robusta beans. The country has only one crop harvested per year, with water becoming an increasingly crucial factor in coffee production due to deforestation and intensive irrigation practices. (Brew a dark roasted Vietnamese 100 % Robusta and add sweetened condensed milk and ice - voila, the famous Vietnamese iced coffee).

3) Colombia
Colombia is the only South American country that boasts ports on both the Atlantic and Pacific oceans. Known for their rich flavor and fine acidity, when thinking of coffee Colombian automatically comes to the mind of most people. Beans of merit-Medellin, Excelso, Supremo.

4) Indonesia
About 90% of coffee produced in the country is done by small farmers. The Indonesian archipelago is one of the earliest producers of coffee apart from India outside of the Arabic world. Beans of merit- Java, Sumatra, Celebes (Sulawesi).

5) India
Established in 1942, the Indian Coffee Board controlled all coffee production. However, the coffee industry was liberalized in 1995 and the marketing of coffee is now a private sector activity. Beans of merit- Mysore, Monsooned Malabar (the green beans are aged in warehouses that are open to the elements).

6) Ethiopia
Ethiopia is the natural home and primary source of the Arabica trees from which all coffee originated. It is estimated that nearly 25% of the total population of its citizens rely on coffee for their livelihood. Beans of merit- Harrar, Ghimbi, Yirgacheffe (Sidamo).

7) Honduras
For a long period of time Honduran coffee did not fetch a good price- therefore many coffees were smuggled across the border into Guatemala and sold as such. That practice has seen a sharp drop and Honduras is reaping the rewards. Beans of merit- All coffees are classified by the altitude at which they are grown- Central Standard, High Grown, and Strictly High Grown (SHG).

8) Peru
Peru is one of the world's foremost producers of organic coffee. Some growers have also formed cooperatives which participate in Fair Trade practices. A very mild coffee with moderate acidity, Peruvian coffee is widely used in dark roasts as well as blends and as a base for flavored coffees. Beans of merit- grown in the Chanchamayo and Urubamba Valleys. The highest grade is AAA.

(9) Guatemala
Guatemala boasts one of the most climatically diverse coffee growing regions in the world. Each of the seven growing regions in the country has its own distinct weather influenced flavor profile which is

enhanced by the care and attention brought by the individual plantation owners. Beans of merit-Antigua, Atitlan, Huehuetenango.

10) Mexico
Most Mexican coffee is grown in the south central (Coatepec) region and southernmost regions of the country (Oaxaca, Chiapas) where the vast majority is grown. They are of high quality, and because of their light body are often used in blends. Mexico is the leader in organic coffee production farms, some of which are Fair Trade. All coffees are classified by the altitude (altura) at which they are grown. Beans of merit- Altura Coatepec, Oaxaca Pluma, Mexican Chiapas.

O.K. But what's Fair Trade?

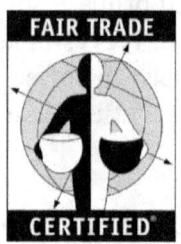

Fair Question.

In coffee producing countries many farms are family owned. Many small farm owners struggle to make enough money from their harvests to live on due to the total costs involved in maintaining their farms, from planting and fertilizing, to labor production. If a fair price cannot be reached for their harvested green beans at market, an entire years' worth of work can be for naught- sometimes to the point of the farmer not being able to grow coffee.

To aid these individuals, an organization was established which is known as Fair Trade International. The organization helps the farmers get a fair price for their green beans so they can continue to grow their coffee and feed their families. Several criteria are involved which guarantee the farmers will get a set (fair) price for their harvest. They include a requirement that the farmers belong to cooperatives or associations that are controlled by their members. Companies that import green beans must agree to team up with the cooperatives and purchase coffee directly from them, cutting out any middlemen. The farms themselves must be environmentally friendly. If the criteria are met the farmer can even access pre-harvest funds from the Fair Trade organization to ensure a good crop. Many organic farms that produce green beans are involved with Fair Trade. The Fair Trade International organization helps farmers worldwide in all of the coffee growing regions throughout the bean belt.

The bean belt regions can be broken up into three parts of the world, these being...

Region 1
Mexico, Central and South America and the Caribbean

This area produces the most coffee out of the three regions. Brazil and Colombia are heavy hitters, with Mexico, Costa Rica and Guatemala also contributing.

Acidity- medium to high
Body- light to medium
Characteristics- can be mild, well balanced, sweet, intense, tangy.

Region 2
Africa and the Middle-East

The most popular coffees from this area are produced in Kenya and Ethiopia. From the Arabian Peninsula comes Arabian Mocha, one of the oldest and finest of the world's coffees.

Acidity- medium to high
Body- medium to full
Characteristics- can be fragrant, fruity, wine-like, citrusy.

Region 3
Southeast Asia

The most popular coffees from this area are exported from the Indonesian islands of Java, Sumatra and Sulawesi (Celebes). Also a player in this field is Vietnam, however they produce mostly Robusta coffee.

Acidity- low
Body- full to heavy
Characteristics- earthy, smooth, chocolaty, robust.

The Civet and the Kopi Luwack

High on a mountain in Southeast Asia on the Indonesian island of Sumatra, a furry bean bandit is foraging for a meal. The intended target? Fresh coffee cherries, his favorite pulpy meal. Under the cover of darkness he roams about, searching for only the ripest red cherries available. When he has had his fill, nature takes its course and the old adage what goes in must come out is brought to fruition. The undigested green coffee beans are unceremoniously pooped into the dirt where for reasons unknown local residents gather them up.

Who is this long tailed marauder? A civet, or more appropriately, an Asian Palm Civet. He is a small, very furry animal resembling a weasel or cat, who lives his life high in the treetops.

The reason the locals gather the clumps of excrement encased green beans goes back many years to the early 1600's when the Dutch owned most of the coffee plantations in Indonesia. The Dutch cultivated and exported all of the crop, leaving no quality coffee for the workers. The local residents, craving their caffeine, took to gathering up the clumps of feces covered beans deposited by the Civet for themselves. They would wash away the feces then sun dry and roast the beans. The unique flavor of the finished coffee is brought about by enzymes in the digestive tract of the Civet.

The finished coffee (named Kopi Luwak) is said to be smooth and earthy with a distinctive taste unlike any other. It is very rare and thus costly. The name for the coffee is derived from the Indonesian words for coffee (Kopi) and palm civet (Luwak). Most of the Kopi Luwak gathered today is consumed by the Japanese, however if you are willing to pay the price you can find it on the market.

Meanwhile, on another island in the Indonesian archipelago, a macaque monkey is also foraging for a meal. On the island of Sulawesi, he wanders through the lowland rainforest searching for cacao (chocolate) trees growing under the forest canopy. Upon finding his target he grasps a cacao pod and breaking through its wall and pulp, eats the sugary mucilage as well as the cacao beans contained within. After breaking open as many pods as it takes to satisfy his hunger, nature takes its course and the old adage what goes in must come out is brought to fruition. The undigested cacao beans are unceremoniously pooped into the dirt and dispersed throughout the rainforest, taking root as future cacao trees.

Cacao-The Other Bean

"The superiority of chocolate, both for health and nourishment, will soon give it the same preference over tea and coffee in America which it has in Spain."
-Thomas Jefferson.

Chocolate.

The name alone conjures up images, thoughts and impressions. Childhood memories of your favorite dessert. A gift of kindness to your sweetheart or loved one. Cooling down a hot afternoon with a cone or heating up the night with a chocolate infused aperitif. Chocolate is a simple indulgence that has found its way into the lives of millions of people. Just try to imagine a world without it. No chocolate Easter eggs. Only hard candy in your Halloween bag. Not a Café Mocha in sight.

Chocolate is one of those things that we unfortunately take for granted. Like breathing. It has been in our lives since our earliest thoughts were formed. Can't eat the fries without the chocolate shake. Order white milk in the cafeteria? I think not. Candy bars? Forget about it. I mean where would Charlie be without his Wonka bar? Probably still at home with his mother looking after Grandpa Joe. But Charlie found his golden ticket, which was appropriately encased in chocolate. Life is like that- searching for the elusive ticket that holds the all of the answers. However, even if you never find them, you can still enjoy a sweet chocolaty treat every day.

Chocolate in its purist form is not sweet. Traced back to its earliest origins (perhaps as early as 1500 B.C.) in Mesoamerica, an area that today encompasses Mexico and much of Central America, it was known as Xocolatl (sho ko la tull- choc o late), or bitter water. Xocolatl was made by roasting and grinding (like coffee) the seeds of the cacao pod and adding hot water to the resulting paste. (grinding cacao beans produces a thick paste due to the cocoa butter contained in them). The Mayans and later the Aztecs adopted the bitter brew and drinking it was as much a part of their lives as eating solid chocolate is in modern times.

In the year 1519 the Spanish explorer Hernando Cortes arrived in Mexico with an armada of soldiers. Two short years later, the Spanish had conquered the Aztecs and claimed their land for Spain. The popularity of cacao was not lost on Cortes, however his men found the drink to bitter to swallow. The islands of the Caribbean held a perfect resource- cane sugar, which was later added to the brew to sweeten it. In 1528 Cortes returned to Spain where he presented his discovery from the new world to King Charles V. The world's love of chocolate had begun.

Did You Know?

Chocoholic is a new phrase that recently came into being. It refers to someone who craves or is very fond of eating chocolate.

George Cadbury made a great fortune producing drinking chocolate as an alternative to alcohol.

Research proves that people who eat dark chocolate live almost a year longer than those who abstain- adopt this as your personal motto.

The preferred ice cream topping is chocolate syrup. No surprise there.

There are three types of chocolate, milk, white, and dark. Milk chocolate is preferred by 80% of the world's population.

Chocolate contains caffeine. However, you would have to eat fourteen (1.5 oz.) bars of milk chocolate to get the same amount of caffeine that you would find in an 8 ounce cup of coffee.

Dark chocolate contains more caffeine than milk chocolate. Given the previous ratio, it would take four dark bars to give you the same amount of caffeine that you would find in an 8 ounce cup of coffee.

One plain milk chocolate candy bar has more protein than a banana.

The first chocolate chip cookie was invented in the early 1930's in

Massachusetts by Ruth Wakefield who along with her husband Kenneth owned the Toll House Inn.

German chocolate cake owes its name to an American chocolate maker named Sam German, and did not originate in Germany.

Chocolate is the only edible substance that melts at around 93° F, just below body temperature. Solid at room temperature, immediately after placing a piece of chocolate on your tongue, it will begin to melt.

Every year on February 14th, Japanese girls give chocolate hearts to their loved ones. The courtesy is exchanged by the men one month later on Howaito, also known as White Day when the women receive white chocolate.

An overwhelming number of people (76%) eat their chocolate bunny starting with his ears.

In Holland, the feast of St. Nicholas is celebrated on December 6th. The children leave their shoes out the evening before so Sinterklaas can fill them up with chocolate money.

In Washington D.C. a highlight of the holiday decorations has become the white chocolate replica of the White House. A tradition since the 1960s, today visitors will find this delicious architectural feat, which can weigh up to 300 pounds and take months to create, displayed in the State Dining Room.

In one year, the world produces 3 million tons of cacao beans, which is less than half of the coffee bean crop. Long live the cacao (and the coffee) bean.

An Enlightening Timeline

Of The Cacao Bean

Circa 1200 B.C. - 400 B.C.
It is widely believed that the Olmec, the earliest known people to inhabit Mesoamerica were the first to cultivate cacao. The Olmec, or more precisely Olmecatl, which in the ancient Aztec language means rubber people, were prolific farmers. Although they cultivated cacao, their primary crops were maize (corn), beans and squash. They were known as rubber people because of their practice of extracting latex from the rubber trees growing in the region and mixing it with the juice of a local vine (morning glory) to create rubber. Taken from the Olmec language, the word kakawa was later translated to the present day word cacao.

400 B.C. - 1100 A.D.
The Olmec's use of cacao is later adopted by the Mayans who inhabit the same region of Mesoamerica (Southern Mexico and Central America). They become enthralled with the bean, incorporating its use into daily life not only through consumption, but through hierarchy, currency, religion, and sacred rituals.

Hierarchy
In the earliest Mayan culture the daily consumption of cacao was restricted only to the elite. The common farmer, merchant, or laborer could only enjoy the beverage during ceremonies or festivals. During these rituals the ruling monarch would preside and perform the Priestly duties. Ceremonial pottery was designed by artisans specifically for this purpose. Ancient tombs have been discovered

containing pottery depicting the cacao bean and its preparation.

Currency

Since the king had absolute control over all of cacao production, using cacao beans as money made perfect sense. When the value of the cacao dropped due to overproduction, he would simply take more beans off of the market and place them in his store rooms. This kept the value of the currency stable and the economy healthy. It also increased the kings wealth and power.

Religion

Cacao played a large part in the myth of the Mayans creation. They believed that their Gods created man from maize, cacao and other nourishing plants. In their belief the cacao tree was given to them directly by the Gods and the cacao pods were their Gods personal gift to human beings. Chocolate was considered the blood of the earth, closely related to their very own life blood, thus related in a sacred manner.

Sacred Rituals

To the Mayans, cacao pods symbolized life and fertility from birth through death. Children were baptized with rain water infused with ground cacao and flowers. At engagement and wedding ceremonies, they honored their Gods with a bitter drink made from the ground cacao, crushed annatto seeds and water. At the time of death, it was presented at the burial and the subject was laid to rest ensuring comfort in the afterlife.

Migrating from Central America to the northern portions of South America, the Mayans established the first known cacao plantations in history. Their territory stretched from the Yucatan Peninsula in Mexico to the Pacific coast of Guatemala.

1200's

The Aztecs, a tribe of wandering nomads, arrive from the north and begin to settle in the Valley of Mexico. The Aztecs begin trade with the Mayans. Their goods likely included jade and animal skins while the Mayans dealt extensively with cacao and spices.Over time, cacao becomes as highly prized in Aztec customs and tradition as it is in the

Mayan, including their belief system. They believe that their God, Quetzalcoatl, brought cacao to earth from paradise as a gift specifically for them.

As with the Mayans, cacao is at first used only by Aztec nobility and the upper class. They continue the tradition of only drinking it at ceremonial events, however they flavor their brew with vanilla beans and black pepper.

For nourishment, Aztec warriors carry small cakes comprised of cacao and maize when on journeys and at war, re-constituting the cakes with water to make an early version of instant hot chocolate.

1300's- 1400's
The Aztecs establish a monarchy in 1376, naming Acamapichtli as their first King. He becomes the founder of the Aztec imperial dynasty. Acamapichtli wants to conquer all of the lands that he can along with all of the people who reside in them, however his main objective is not to kill people but to integrate the prisoners into his

own society. King Acamapichtli exacts a tribute from all of his native followers along with his conquered peoples. A tribute is actually a tax which could be submitted to him in the form of many types of goods (one of which is cacao beans)- paid to him by citizens who were conquered in the main cacao growing regions.

As time passed, more expensive goods could still be accepted as tribute but cacao beans became the major form of tax and currency. By subjugating the Mayans and other native peoples, the Aztecs strengthened their supremacy throughout Mexico. Records still exist showing the details of cacao deliveries that were imposed on all of the conquered tribes.

King Acamapichtli rules for twenty years, and upon his death passes the throne onto his successor. By the end of 1400 A.D., the Aztec Empire covers nearly all of Mexico and extends well into the southern regions of Central America. The capital city was located at Tenochtitlan, which today is the site of modern day Mexico City.

1500's
Spanish explorer Hernan Cortes and his armada depart from the island of Cuba and arrive on the shores of the Gulf of Mexico in the Yucatan Peninsula in 1519. They construct a settlement called La Villa de la Vera Cruz (the village of the true cross). The encampment will later be known as Veracruz. At this time Montezuma is the ruling king of the Aztecs.

Cortes is on a mission to conquer lands for Spain. Two years after arriving on the Yucatan Peninsula, Cortes and his men (along with native dissidents) defeat King Montezuma and his warriors. This is largely due to the fact that their numbers combined with modern weaponry gave them a distinct advantage. They take over the city of Tenochtitlan, and Cortes is soon known as the Governor and Captain General of New Spain.

Cortes returns to Spain in 1528 with a cargo of cacao beans which he presents to King Charles V. Drinking the brew gains ever increasing popularity as the practice of adding sugar becomes the standard. The Spanish dominate the cacao industry for many years. Because of its profitability, the nobles keep the details of processing cacao private. The processing is done by monks up until the year 1580, when a chocolate production plant is built in Spain.

To supply the demand for chocolate, Cortes is instrumental in the development of cacao bean plantations across Mexico, Trinidad, Haiti and the rest of the Caribbean. The harbor of Veracruz, the settlement founded by Cortes, becomes Mexico's most important port of export.

1600's
Cacao is introduced to the French court by a fourteen year old Spanish princess, Anne of Austria, the daughter of Philip III of Spain when she marries France's Louis XIII. The custom of drinking sweetened chocolate is embraced by the French.

Aided by the growing popularity of drinking cocoa by the French society, chocolate expands rapidly throughout Europe, becoming popular in England, Italy, Germany, Switzerland, and Holland.

The custom of not only drinking but eating chocolate is now being experimented with in the form of chocolate infused rolls and cakes. The earliest handmade solid chocolates are produced. Known as lozenges or pastilles, they rapidly become popular.

The first English Chocolate House is opened by a Frenchman. He is responsible for the first advertisements for chocolate drinks to be seen in London. It was in this period that the English improved the drink by adding milk. The chocolate houses also sold a pressed cake from which the drink could be made at home.

The first cacao plantations in Brazil are established. As time goes on Brazil will become one of the prominent producers of cacao in the chocolate industry.

1700's
The son of Anne of Austria, heir to the throne Louis XIV, carries on the infatuation of chocolate when he is crowned. At Versailles he

creates a position in his Court appropriately entitled Royal Chocolate Maker to the King. Louis hands the tradition down to his own son who becomes as much of a chocolate lover as his father.

Cacao arrives in many European ports from plantations throughout Mexico, Central and South America, and the Caribbean. Plantation workers harvest, ferment, and dry the beans for export overseas. Once arriving in European ports, the beans would be ground by hand. As supply and demand increased, so the method of production needed to change.

As the world enters the industrial age, a French inventor by the name of Dubuisson creates a table to grind the cacao beans into chocolate paste. Although it still requires physical manpower it makes processing cocoa more efficient and less tiring on the workers.

In Bristol, England, a factory is opened that uses the newest technology available. It uses steam driven hydraulic machinery to process cacao beans into cocoa eliminating the need for hands on methods and makes way for mass production. Some years later, in 1847, the same chocolate factory, Fry's, molds the first ever chocolate bar suitable for widespread consumption.

The first factory to produce chocolate in the New World opens just outside of Boston in Milton, Massachusetts. It is located in a reclaimed water driven grist mill on the Neponset River. As the sale of their product (Baker's Chocolate) increases, production is moved across the river to Dorchester.

It was at this time that the first advertisements for chocolate in America appear in the Boston Gazette and also the Country Journal. From this point on chocolate production increases even more rapidly throughout the world but particularly more so in America where it is embraced from the east to the west coast.

1800's
With the industrial revolution well under way, chocolate in both production and consumption has come into its own. With the ever increasing number of cacao plantations and chocolate factories the

price of chocolate begins to stabilize and the commodity that had previously been only for the elite becomes a more affordable and widely consumed treat.

Due to production and consumption, technology is increasing in leaps and bounds. In order to aid the chocolate makers in their quest for an even more saleable product, inventors and tool makers are tinkering away in machine shops all over the world. Along with improving on the existing chocolate making contraptions, two additions of major importance are introduced that chocolate makers still implement today.

1828 The Cocoa Press.

Conrad Van Houten, a Dutch chemist, is issued a patent in Amsterdam for a machine that extracts the natural cocoa butter from the ground roasted cacao beans using a hydraulic press. After the cocoa butter was pressed from the cacao, it left a cake that was ground and with the addition of alkaline salts made a powder that would mix more readily with water or milk. The process is known as dutching.

1879 The Conching Machine.

Rodolphe Lindt, a chocolatier from a wealthy family in the town of Bern, Switzerland founds a factory. He is much more interested in producing quality chocolate than in making money. Lindt develops a machine that heats and grinds the cacao beans for up to seventy two hours. The grinding rollers resemble conch shells, thus the method. The result is a finer, glossier chocolate, much less grainy than its counterparts. Lindt calls the resulting finished product chocolat fondant.

Seizing the demand for chocolate along with the available technology, emerging companies are founded worldwide and begin to make contributions to the burgeoning chocolate industry. Some of these earliest pioneers exist to this day and you may very well recognize them. They include in order of appearance, 1831 Cadbury's (England), 1845 Lindt (Switzerland), 1852 Ghirardelli (United States), 1894 Hershey's (United States), and in 1899 Toblerone (Switzerland).Vying for market share, these companies along with many others begin to transform chocolate and to develop many new varieties. Their main focus is on solid chocolates.

In Switzerland, Daniel Peter and Henri Nestle combine cocoa powder and cocoa butter with sugar and dried milk powder to produce the first milk chocolate bars. In local food shops people are now discovering not only pure chocolate treats, but bonbons made of chocolate with a fondant, fruit, or nut center.

It is in the 1800's when cacao plantations are being established in Ghana, West Africa. These original homesteads have grown and today West Africa (the Ivory Coast) is one of the main producers of cacao.

1900's
Riding the wave of the newest modern technology, chocolate maker's sail into the twentieth century. Taking advantage of a breakthrough first started in the automobile industry, they install assembly lines and conveyor belts, increasing their production levels tenfold.

The devil is in the details. Although chocolate has been used in baking since the 1600's, it is not until the mid-1800's when baking chocolate becomes refined that baking with chocolate becomes more refined as well. Around the time people were celebrating New Year's Eve and the arrival of the year 1900, recipes for Devil's Food cake begin to show up in the cookbooks. It was all the rage, in fact the Modern Women of America magazine (published in 1913) had no less than 23 variations for making it. The earlier version of the cake, Angels Food, was light and airy, fit for an angel. Devils Food was sinfully dark and rich. And so the progression of mankind. Angel's food belongs to the nineteenth century but devil's food belongs to the twentieth.

Chocolate bars move into the forefront as a grab and go item. Retailers install display racks to implement and showcase the tasty treats. Many of the bars sold today were born in this era including the Hershey milk chocolate bar which was among the earliest. So inspired were the townsfolk of Derry Church, Pennsylvania, that in 1906 they change the name of their town to Hershey to honor the company's founder Milton S. Hershey who built his factory there.

In 1912, the Belgian chocolatier Jean Neuhaus creates the first bite-sized filled bonbon chocolates, which he named pralines. The hard chocolate covered shell (or couverture) enabled liquid fillings to be used for the first time. Previously only solid centers such as caramel could be used or the liquid filling would have leaked out.

With the advance of the chocolate bar, the choice of ingredients multiplies. Available are bars made with fruit, nuts, caramel, fondant, and nougat.

The roaring Twenties are seen as the highest point in the chocolate bar industry as it is estimated that thousands of types of candy bars were created in that decade- appearing on retailers' shelves to satisfy the consumers ever growing demand and infatuation with the confection.

In the early 1930's, Ruth Wakefield, the owner of the Toll House Inn in Whitman, Massachusetts was baking for her guests. She was using an old time Colonial butter drop cookie recipe. The recipe called for powdered bakers' chocolate which she didn't have, so she substituted a broken up Nestlé chocolate bar in its place. The chocolate stayed in pieces, not creating the chocolate flavored dough she expected. Her guests were delighted with the chip filled cookie and when the recipe was printed in a Boston newspaper the cookie became an overnight sensation.

Henri Nestlé took note of the Wakefield phenomenom and began scoring his chocolate bars to make them easier to break. In 1939 he fulfilled a brainstorm and the first bags of chocolate chips rolled off the assembly line.

2000's

There is a well-known adage that states that everything old is new again. As mankind presses steadily onward into the twenty first century through modernization and technology, we look forward to the new with a mixture of wonder and apprehension while still clinging to the old with feelings of nostalgia and remorse. Some people embrace technology- like the scientist or physicist who strives to change the world in a laboratory. Others look backward rather than forward- like the archaeologist getting his hands dirty sifting through history at the very point of its origin.

Chocolate manufacturers in today's world have to run their facilities like laboratories. Many elements are involved in taking the cacao from its original state to the finished product. To begin, quality control personnel must inspect the incoming beans to ensure they are superior and are the finest available. Consistency on the assembly line is of the utmost importance. Precision instruments are used to track temperature and moisture levels and regulate the timing of automated processes. The final product must again be inspected and only then can it be packaged for delivery. Every time you purchase your favorite treat, it tastes exactly the same.

Entrepreneurial chocolatiers who specialize in old school hand crafted confections continue to grow with an amazing assortment of new delicacies. They have created their own niche market with chocolate shops and cafés where they ply their off the wall edible art. Calling them artisans is not an understatement. Using such unusual ingredients as bacon or cheese they explore the savory side of the bean. At the other end of the scale, candied violet or lavender petals flower the sweet notes. Would you like some salt in your chocolate? Pepper or cayenne? How about a chocolate covered onion? The limits are endless and only held in bounds by the crafts-mens imaginations

Even today, harvesting cacao pods is very labor intensive. Less than 5% of cacao is grown on large plantations, thus the main majority of the world's production comes from small farms. On some farms the entire family, along with any friends or neighbors available help out. The pods are cut from the tree and collected in baskets, then split open by hand to separate the beans from the sweet, white, pulpy mucilage.

In 2007, archaeologists excavating a site in Puerto Escondido, Honduras found evidence of the cultivation and use of cacao dating back from about 1100 to 1400 B.C. The type of vessel and the residue contained in it indicates that the sweet white pulp around the cacao beans was being used as a source of fermentable sugars for an alcoholic drink.

Africa is the largest exporter of cacao beans. Four major West African cocoa producers, the Ivory Coast, Ghana, Nigeria and Cameroon, together account for about two-thirds of world cacao production. Outside of West Africa, the major producers of cacao are Indonesia, Brazil, Malaysia, Ecuador, and the Dominican Republic. Whether you eat or drink your chocolate, a whole worlds worth of time and effort has brought us to the point where we are now.

Chocolate bars and chocolate candies, chocolate truffles and chocolate chews, chocolate barks and chocolate fudge. Dark chocolate and hot chocolate, milk chocolate and chocolate milk, sweet chocolate and bitter chocolate, chocolate creams and chocolate crisps.

Chocolate cake and chocolate pie, chocolate mousse and chocolate pudding. Nuts and nougat. Fruit and fondant. Caramel and malted milk. White and dark chocolate bunnies, dark chocolate and milk chocolate Santa's, chocolate hearts and chocolate skeletons. Chocolate coins and chocolate calendars. Fresh from the candy store or fresh out of the oven, chocolate reigns supreme.

From The Flower Buds

To Your Taste Buds

The first outsider to drink chocolate was Christopher Columbus, who reached Nicaragua on his fourth voyage to the Americas in 1502 while searching for a sea route to the spices of the East. Columbus wasn't impressed with the drink and virtually dismissed his findings. When he returned to Spain, the beans were overlooked in favor of the other treasures on board his ship. It wasn't for another twenty years when Cortes arrived on the scene that chocolate found its fame.

The trees that were in existence when Columbus arrived in the New World sprang from seedlings that would soon populate the earth. The earliest trees are believed to have been discovered anywhere from 1200-1500 B.C. growing wild along the rivers in Central America and all the way to the Amazon basin. When Columbus arrived, cacao trees had already been domesticated for as long as two thousand years.

The Tree- Theobroma Cacao

The name of the cacao tree, (Theobroma cacao) literally means Food of the Gods- taken from the Greek 'theo' meaning deity (or God), and 'broma' meaning food. It is an evergreen, which means it keeps its leaves yearlong. The initial shrub can grow to heights of over fifty feet, however on commercial plantations it is kept trimmed for the ease of harvesting.

Cacao trees begin to bear fruit when they are three to four years old, producing clusters of small white or light pink odorless blossoms that flower continuously throughout the year. Of the thousands of five petaled blossoms, less than 10% will develop into cacao pods. The blossoms are pollinated by tiny flies called midges and if not pollinized, will die within 24 hours. After the blossoms are pollinized, small green pods appear. Taking four to five months to mature, they can take up to eight months to fully ripen to a bright red, yellow, or purple pod. Ripe cacao pods range from eight to fourteen inches in length and are roughly the size of a cantaloupe. Weighing about a pound, they are football shaped with grooved sides. Inside the pod is a layer of white pulp protecting a sweet sticky mucilage that has anywhere from 20-60 seeds (cacao beans) embedded in it. Each tree yields approximately 20-30 pods per year.

The most unusual fact about the tree is the fact that the pods not only grow on the lower branches of the tree, but

directly out of the trunk itself. The production of flowers directly on the trunk itself is known as cauliflory, and is uniquely different from other trees that produce flowers and fruit only at the end of the twigs on their branches. Cacao trees flourish only between 20 degrees N. and 20 degrees S. of the equator (the twenty-twenty zone) and can grow at elevations from sea level to 3000 ft., however most of the world's crop is grown in areas of less than 1000 ft. above sea level.

The four most important factors when growing cacao are shade, temperature and humidity, and rainfall.

Shade
Having originated in the rain forests which provide natural shade, cacao trees cannot endure exposure to tropical sun. Shading is of the utmost importance- especially in a young plants early years. They must be grown in the shade of other trees, usually under banana trees, palms or rubber plants. The trees take full advantage of the indirect sunlight in the shadow.

Temperature and Humidity

The trees thrive in relatively high temperatures, generally between 65-86 ° F. The heat combined with the humidity is an integral component for the healthy development of cacao trees. In cacao producing countries, the relative humidity as a rule is quite high, often reaching 100% during the day, and falling to 70-80% overnight.

Rainfall

The overall health and the amount of cacao beans a tree produces on a yearly basis is affected by rainfall more than by any other climatic factor. The trees do not tolerate drought well and require rain that is distributed evenly throughout the year. A minimum of 39 inches of rain a year is required with the optimum being 59-79 inches. Because of the tree's shallow root system, well-drained soil is also required, as well as protection from the wind.

There are three different varieties of cacao trees from which most chocolate is produced today. They are Criollo, Forastero and Trinitario.

Criollo (Spanish translation: Créole)

Criollo is the original strain or variety of cacao tree and was grown by the Mayans. They are grown in Mexico, South and Central America, and Indonesia. Often referred to as the 'prince of cocoas', it is considered to produce the best chocolate available (some of the finest is grown in Ecuador).Its pods are softer, thin and lighter colored, and its beans have a naturally mild flavor. A fragile plant, the variety accounts for only 1% to 5% of world production due to its vulnerability to insects and disease. It also yields smaller harvests.

Forastero (Spanish translation: Foreigner)

Forastero is a variety of cacao that is more resistant to disease and pests and therefore more productive than the Criollo. Originally grown in South America, it is now the predominant variety cultivated in

Africa- consequently accounting for nearly 80% of world production. The trees produce thicker pods and the beans have a strong chocolate taste. The quality of the chocolate it produces is mainstream, therefore it is widely used in the mass production of almost everything chocolate.

: Criollo beans are slightly rounded and yellowish to white in color. They are very aromatic, just slightly bitter and have a delicate flavor.

: Forastero beans are smaller than Criollo beans, flattened on the side, have a dark reddish-brown to violet color and a sharper flavor.

Trinitario (No translation, thought to mean bred in Trinidad)

Trinitario is a variety of cacao tree that is a natural biological hybrid between the Criollo and the Forastero, which is to say a strain that was cross bred. It originated in Trinidad where the Spanish colonists had established plantations. Because it is a hybrid, it contains qualities from both of its parents. It has smoother pods and flavorful beans. The chocolate it produces can range from average to superior and represents roughly 15% of world production.

Cacao farmers have to be vigilant to protect their trees, which are susceptible to many naturally occurring forces of nature such as weather, insects and disease. The best way to maintain a cacao field is the process known as pruning, or macheté technology. The objective of pruning is to give the cacao tree a structure that will help to not only increase its general health, but to maximize its production capacity. The leaves are trimmed and any dead branches are cleared away. Ideally, a cacao tree should be maintained at a height of approximately fourteen to fifteen feet for the ease of everyday management and for easier harvesting.

Pruning regularly allows the plant to receive more sunlight which not only strengthens the formation of new leaves, it increases the production of blossoms and growth of the pods themselves. A well maintained pruned tree is healthier, stronger and better equipped to fight pests and disease. Pruning generally takes place twice a year, in early summer and again in late fall.

Harvesting Cacao

Because the tree flowers continuously and bears fruit at the same time, it is conceivable that harvesting could be done almost year round. However, commercial growers count on two crops a year, the largest being in the late fall starting in September and peaking around November, while the spring season centers on April and continues into late June.

Ripe pods are gathered every few weeks during the peak season. It is important to harvest the pods only when they are fully ripe because if the pod is unripe, the beans themselves will have a low cocoa butter content, or there will be insufficient sugars in the sweet sticky mucilage for proper fermentation. Low cocoa butter content or an insufficient amount of natural sugar will result in an inferior flavor profile in the finished chocolate.

The ripe pods are harvested by hand with a knife or macheté by the cacao pickers who take a great amount of care, since the growth of new stems and leaves start where the ripe pod was removed. Higher pods are reached with a blade pole- again  with care so as not to damage nearby buds and blossoms.

Because the tree is frail and its root system so shallow, harvesters cannot risk damaging it by climbing to reach the pods on the higher branches. It requires training and experience to know by appearance which fruit is ripe and ready to be cut, and it is not possible to harvest the pods by machine. The pods are collected in large baskets and piled up ready for splitting.

Fermenting Cacao

After harvesting, the pods are split open to remove the cacao seeds. Most farmers have their workers group the pods in large piles close to the cacao fields themselves and split them there. Sometimes the pods are transported to a fermenting facility. If the pods are opened near the planted areas, the discarded husks can be distributed throughout the fields to compost and be used as future fertilizer.

The best way of splitting open a pod is to hit it directly in the middle causing it to split so that it can be broken into two halves. Most skilled workers use their macheté to accomplish this. Once split, the creamy white mucilage containing the seeds can be scooped out by hand or with a wooden utensil onto a bed of banana leaves or a tarp. Another layer of leaves or another tarp will be used to cover the heap (a mixture of seeds and mucilage). The entire heap will ferment from two to seven days to stop the cacao seed from germinating, dissolve the mucilage and to enhance the finished chocolates flavors. During this time frame the heap will be stirred periodically to allow aeration and also to increase the naturally occurring enzymes activity in the cacao seeds.

Before fermentation, the cacao seeds (beans) taste almost nothing like chocolate. The main reason for fermenting the mucilage/cacao bean mix is to mellow out the beans, eliminating any acidic or bitter tastes, and to increase the complexity of the final flavor. The mucilage itself contains mostly water with 10-15% sugars. High sugar content favors the growth of yeast and bacteria, which in turn create heat under the covering of the leaves or tarp. The resulting heat activates the natural enzymes in the beans, stops them from germinating, and creates the chemical compounds that give the beans their chocolate flavor and color.

The length of fermentation varies depending on the bean type . Forastero beans require about five days and Criollo beans from two to three. At the end of the fermentation process, the mucilage has completely broken down and drained away and the beans are ready to be dried.

In an industrial environment, a series of strong wooden boxes equipped with drainage holes are used, which allow air and liquid to pass through them. The boxes are placed in steps- the

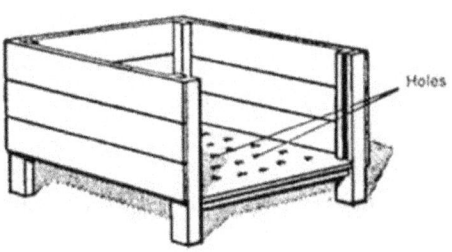

Holes

first box filled with fresh mucilage covered beans. After a few days the content is mixed and transferred to the next box, a process which is repeated until the last box is reached. In four to six days, box fermentation reaches the same result as the traditional heap fermentation process. Some say that the wooden boxes enhance the cacaos natural enzymes fermenting activity and increase flavor in the beans. After the fermentation process, the moisture content of the cacao is approximately 60%, and this must be reduced to 7 – 7.5% before the cacao beans can be stored, sold or transported. The main reason for drying the beans to this percentage of moisture is to ensure that there is no chance of mold.

Drying Cacao

Drying must be carried out carefully to ensure that the beans maintain the flavor profile developed during fermentation. The process should take place slowly- from one to two weeks depending on the weather. During this time the bean changes from a reddish brown to a darker brown color. The rate of drying is critical to the final flavor and quality of the chocolate itself. If the beans are dried too quickly the chemical reactions started in fermentation are cut short and the beans can be acidic, with a bitter flavor. If done too slowly, molds and other unpleasant flavors can develop. Properly dried cacao beans can be stored for a period of up to 4- 5 years. There are two methods for drying beans- sun drying and artificial drying.

Sun Drying
The method of sun drying involves spreading the fermented beans out on mats, trays or concrete floors in the sun. As the beans dry they are raked and all traces of remaining mucilage is removed. Drying also completes the oxidation of any remaining acetic acid, mellowing the beans. Visually, any defective beans can be removed. Raking periodically also ensures uniformity of drying from bean to bean. Some farmers have patios with removable roofs in case of rain, others simply cover the cacao with a tarp. Sun drying is by far the preferred method used by growers.

Artificial Drying
Artificial drying is an alternative method available in countries where

there is a lack of pronounced dry periods after harvesting and fermentation. Beans can be artificially dried with the same concept used by a clothes dryer- hot air. This method dries the beans a lot more quickly, however it can result in poor quality chocolate with a smoky or slightly burnt flavor characteristic. Artificial drying is most often used when sun drying has reduced the moisture content to approximately 20%, finishing the process to reach the desired goal of 7% moisture.

Cacao beans that have been adequately dried and warehoused are usually shipped by sea. Now referred to as *raw cocoa* and traditionally exported in jute bags, raw cocoa is now increasingly loaded onto ships in bulk containers. While shipping in bulk significantly reduces handling costs, shipment in jute bags either directly in the ship's hold or inside of containers is still commonly found.

Before arrival at the factory and while in transshipment, the first quality control inspection has taken place while the raw cocoa was in port. From its port of entry it is trucked to the receiving manufacturer. Manufacturers who import raw cocoa keep careful track of each shipment they receive. Every shipment is carefully inspected and approved, adhering to the strict quality control guidelines that will continue throughout the entire processing procedure.

First, the beans are separated according to type and country of origin. Next, they are carefully cleaned to remove any foreign debris, and then they are graded and sorted by size. It is at this time a manufacturer may combine a blend that is specific only to them. The raw cocoa is now ready for the final steps in becoming chocolate.

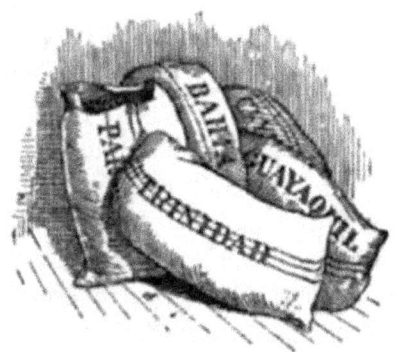

Processing Cacao

Roast, Winnow, Grind, Conch and Temper

To fully grasp the process of roasting and winnowing (shelling), it is best to understand the makeup of the cocoa bean itself. First, there is the outermost seed coat (shell), then the kernel itself (nib). A small corner of the nib itself contains a section called the germ. A safe analysis would comprise of a cocoa bean being 12% shell, 87% nib, and 1% germ.

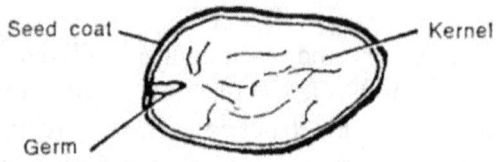

Ideally as much of the shell and the germ should be removed from the nib as possible because the shell is inedible and the germ itself is bitter and contributes bad flavor. The nib is where all of the chocolate is hiding. When roasting cocoa, the entire bean is roasted, shell and all.

Roasting

The key to excellent chocolate flavor is in the roasting. During roasting, flavor molecules that developed during fermentation interact with the heat to produce the desired chocolate taste. When tasted raw, cocoa beans have a bitter almost astringent flavor. By roasting the cocoa, the chemistry of the bean is altered- the acidity is mellowed, and the flavor, color, and aroma of the bean is released. Large rotating ovens roast the beans at temperatures of 250°F or more to release the rich aromas and delicious taste. The roast can last anywhere from forty five minutes to two hours, depending on the temperature level used and different variables such as humidity, size and type of bean, and whether the end product is to be used for ground cocoa or eating chocolate. The flavor acquired by properly fermented and dried cocoa is enhanced by the further loss of moisture and the darkening of the

bean to a rich brown hue. When the cocoa beans have reached the desired roast level, they are poured onto a large cooling table where powerful fans are used to quickly cool them. This effectively stops the roasting process. Blowing cool air over the beans combined with rotating or stirring them ensures that they cool quickly and evenly. The beans (still encased in their brittle shell) are now ready to be winnowed.

The next step is to crack and winnow the cocoa beans, the end result being a separation of the nib, shell and germ. The basic process of winnowing (shelling) involves an initial crack of the bean. The goal of a good crack is to keep the nib as large as possible while simultaneously separating the shell and dislodging the germ.

Once the cooled beans have arrived from the roaster, they enter the winnowing machine. Inside the machine the beans are passed between two large rollers that crack the brittle shells without crushing the nibs. The separated shells and nibs are then sent over a series of vibrating screens that have progressively smaller openings. The vibration causes the heavier nibs to fall through the perforated holes in the screens to be collected while the lighter germ and larger pieces of shell and debris are left behind. The discarded shell and dusty debris are then removed by blasts of forced air as more roasted beans enter the machine. The nibs, now roasted and free of their shells and the germ, are ready to be ground.

...a quick word about cocoa nibs...

If you like dark chocolate, then unprocessed cocoa nibs are definitely for you. They have a complex, bitter, cocoa buttery flavor and can be used in many different ways. Eating them straight from the bag isn't uncommon. Adding them to baked goods or folding them into ice cream is recommended. Topping a green or fruit salad? Why not. Another plus is that they are really good for you. Dark chocolate is

high in antioxidants. Cocoa nibs are as dark and unsweetened as you will find. They are also high in magnesium, chromium, and vitamin C. All of this without any of the calories associated with sweetened chocolate. Hmm.

...a quick word about cocoa shells...

When you are in the process of mulching around your yard, cocoa shell mulch is an option. The roasting process of the cacao beans sterilizes the shells so that they are pure and organic. Many people enjoy the sweet aroma and attractive appearance of the dark cocoa shell mulch. It contains nitrogen, phosphates and potash. On the downside, in hot and humid climates the mulch can develop a harmless mold. This can be removed however, with a simple spray of water and vinegar. Because the shells naturally contain caffeine and theobromine, it may be wise to use the mulch in a fenced yard, as the sweet smell of the cocoa mulch could be attractive to curious dogs and even small amounts of cocoa could be potentially dangerous to an unleashed visitor.

Grinding and Pressing

The nibs themselves are the very essence of the cacao bean, made up of cocoa solids and cocoa butter, the ratio being approximately 47% pure cocoa solids and 53% cocoa butter. The nibs are passed through steel discs or grinding stones where they are ground. As the nibs are crushed, the friction generates enough heat to separate the solids from the butter, liquefying the cocoa butter and creating a substance known as cocoa liquor (cocoa solids suspended in liquid cocoa butter). Cocoa liquor is actually more of a solid than a liquid, in essence a thick, gritty paste. Cocoa liquor is also known as cocoa mass. The mass (basically finely ground cacao beans) is the foundation for all chocolate products. The mass can be used in three ways.

1) If the mass is cooled at this point and hardened into molds, it would form bitter (baking) chocolate;

2) If the mass is pressed, squeezing out all of the existing cocoa butter, the resulting cake (press cake) produced would be pulverized to make cocoa powder;

3) If the mass is continued to be ground (refined) with the addition of sugar and extra cocoa butter, it would result in sweet (eating) chocolate.

Eating chocolate- The amount of sugar added to the mass or whether it was mixed with powdered milk will result in either dark chocolate or milk chocolate. White chocolate is made by combining the extracted cocoa butter with milk, sugar and vanilla, it contains none of the cocoa mass (chocolate liquor) at all.

Conching and Tempering
When the cocoa mass is used to make sweet (eating) chocolate, the ingredients include the cocoa mass itself , additional cocoa butter, sugar, a flavor component such as vanilla, and an emulsifier, usually lecithin (lecithin is derived from soy beans).The mass continues to be ground and becomes more and more refined. (The process is actually known as refining). During the process, cocoa mass and sugar are mixed and ground gradually becoming finer and smoother as more cocoa butter is added to the mix along with the emulsifier and flavoring agents. The refined mixture is then introduced to the conching machine.

With the use of heavy rollers, the conching machine grinds, heats, mixes, agitates and aerates the refined cocoa making it smoother and smoother as more time passes. Even after refining, liquid chocolate prior to conching has an uneven and gritty texture. The conching process further breaks down the cocoa and sugar, resulting in particles that are smaller than the tongue can detect, hence the smooth feel in the mouth. Depending on the quality of the desired chocolate, conching can take anywhere from a few hours to a few days. When the smooth and velvety finished chocolate comes out of the conching machine, it has been fully processed and is ready to use in various ways.

The conched liquid chocolate can now be used to make solid shapes by simply pouring it into molds and allowing it to harden. If a hollow figure is desired, a two piece mold is utilized. The chocolate is poured into the bottom half of the mold which is then joined to the top half. The assembled mold is then rotated to disperse the chocolate evenly, then cooled so that the hardened hollow chocolate figure can be removed. This method can also be used for chocolates with liquid centers.

To obtain a liquid center, the chocolate is poured into a single mold which is then rotated so that any excess chocolate drains away. The layer of chocolate that sticks to the mold is solidified by cooling. A liquid filling is then dispensed into the mold and covered with another layer of chocolate which is allowed to harden.

Another method used to make filled chocolates is known as enrobing, or immersing a solid center filling in liquid chocolate and allowing it to harden. The dipped chocolate candies can then be decorated with anything from chocolate swirls to a few grains of sea salt. In a factory setting, the candy centers are transported on a conveyer belt through a liquid chocolate bath to enrobe them, then cooled, boxed and sent out to retailers who provide chocoholics a vast array of confections. In a retail environment they are hand-dipped. Do yourself a favor- find a local shop in your area that makes fresh hand dipped chocolates (or dip them yourself!). The reward will be well worth the effort.

Before molding the chocolate into solid bars or using it to enrobe a filling, it must be tempered. The word "temper" actually refers to the way that the chocolate solidifies. Proper tempering gives the chocolate a glossy bright finish, along with the desired silky texture that results in a smoother melt in your mouth. Tempering is achieved by an alternating process of heating, cooling, and reheating the chocolate within specific temperature guidelines to stabilize the mixture. If not properly tempered the finished chocolate will appear dull and streaky.

Chocolate that has been properly tempered has a uniform finish, along with a distinctive sheen. If properly handled, it will maintain its final appearance and taste. If improperly tempered or exposed to heat or moisture, however, it can result in what is known as a chocolate bloom. Bloom is a whitish film that discolors the surface of finished chocolate. Chocolate bloom is caused by the two main reasons that we are all addicted to chocolate for in the first place- fat and sugar.

Fat Bloom

By far the most common type of bloom, fat bloom is caused when the chocolate is exposed to high temperatures. When the chocolate heats up, the cocoa butter melts and separates from the cocoa solids, rising to the surface and creating a whitish gray dust known as a bloom. While fat bloom has a negative effect on appearance, the product remains perfectly safe to eat and can be re-tempered to reach the desired appearance.

Sugar Bloom

Less common than fat bloom, sugar bloom is caused by moisture. It has more of a speckled appearance which is caused by crystallized grains of sugar, rather than an even layer of dusty white on the surface. An excess of moisture actually causes the sugar in the chocolate to crystallize. If there isn't a lot of sugar bloom, the chocolate may actually be salvageable if it is removed. However, if the bloom is more severe, excessive moisture may have caused bacterial growth and the product should most likely be discarded.

Basically, it is safe to say that the key to avoiding chocolate bloom is to store your chocolate safely away from heat and moisture. The flavor of bloomed chocolate is not affected - just your mind set when you eat it. If you still feel uneasy about eating it, take up baking and repurpose any chocolate that has bloomed. Simply melt any chocolate affected by sugar bloom and use it in any recipe that calls for chocolate in a liquid form, or pour it over ice cream. Re-temper chocolate with fat bloom to make chocolate for handmade candies or for dipping cookies or fruit. A new hobby in the kitchen involving chocolate can't hurt, and on the upside you might make some new friends as well.

Homemade Chocolate

When baking with chocolate, many recipes require that the chocolate be melted and then introduced in some way, such as when making certain cookies, a frosting or a filling of some kind. This can be done quite easily in a microwave oven by alternatively melting small pieces of chocolate in a bowl, removing it from the microwave and adding more pieces of chocolate and stirring them in.

Another method of melting chocolate is to use a double boiler or bain-marie (water bath) on the top of your stove. The bain-marie is the preferred method when going a step further in the homemade chocolate process. Melted chocolate is simply that- melted chocolate. If allowed to harden it will be soft and sticky. If you want to make the perfect enrobed (dipped) chocolates at home you have to venture just a little bit further and temper the melted chocolate yourself.

Tempering chocolate simply means heating and cooling melted chocolate so that it dries to a hard, shiny finish- the finished chocolate doesn't melt at room temperature, breaks with a nice snap instead of crumbling apart, and is perfect for coating candies and any other goodies you might choose. Without getting too technical and to understand why we temper, it is best to understand the makeup of chocolate at its simplest level.

Chocolate is made up of cocoa butter crystals. When purchasing chocolate it is usually tempered, hard and shiny with the right crystal structure. If you want to use the chocolate to coat something, you have to melt it. Melting the chocolate destroys a lot of the crystals, and you have to create new ones. Creating new crystals in melted chocolate is a process known as seeding. Confused? Not to worry- all will be clear.

The main reason for tempering chocolate is the quality of the finished product. Properly tempered chocolate has a smooth glossy texture and a distinctive snap when broken. It sets quickly and if using a mold, will come out easily without sticking. When tempering, the number one thing to remember is this- chocolate and water don't mix. If even a little water comes into contact with melted chocolate, the sugar and cacao will immediately absorb the moisture and cause it to clump up. This is known as seizing. If for some reason you are unfortunate enough to experience this- don't fret! Although you can't use seized chocolate for dipping, you can always salvage it by stirring in some solid vegetable shortening. Add the shortening by the tablespoon to the melted chocolate and stir gently until the chocolate has loosened and reached the consistency you want. It can now be used for other recipes that call for melted chocolate.

Tempering Chocolate

Assemble all of your required utensils. These include- the chocolate itself, a saucepan, a glass or metal bowl, a rubber spatula, and a digital thermometer. Make sure that everything is DRY. Remember, chocolate and water don't mix. The saucepan is going to have water in it and the bowl will be sitting on top of it on the stove, so be sure to find a bowl that sits snugly. This will minimize any steam that may try to escape during the tempering process. Begin by putting about an inch of water into a saucepan and bringing it to a simmer (don't boil it).

You can use any quality chocolate in block or bar form, or purchase chocolate wafers specifically made for baking. Don't use prepackaged chocolate chips as they contain additives to keep them from melting- this is why they keep a relatively uniform shape when baked.

Using at least a pound of chocolate, chop it with a knife into small uniform pieces. Put 2/3 of the chocolate pieces into the bowl and put the bowl over the simmering saucepan. Keep the other 1/3 of the chopped chocolate aside. The chocolate you have kept aside will be used to 'seed' later. Stir the chocolate with the rubber spatula continuously until it has all melted smoothly. Melt the chocolate too approximately:

115° F for Dark Chocolate and
110° F for Milk or White Chocolate.

Be sure the thermometer doesn't touch the bottom of the bowl! This will cause an inaccurate reading. When the proper temperature has been reached, remove the bowl from the saucepan and carefully wipe the condensed steam from the bottom. The reserved chocolate can now be stirred bit by bit into the melted chocolate.

The process of adding the reserved chocolate into the hot melted chocolate is known as seeding. The cocoa crystals that were destroyed during the heating process will now be replaced with the seed crystals. Don't be afraid to stir. The stirring process not only cools the chocolate, it also agitates and distributes the crystals more evenly throughout the mixture. The more you stir, the glossier your finished chocolate will be. Stir and melt the seed chocolate until it has reached a temperature of 80° F. If there is remaining seed chocolate, remove it- you can eat or use it later. When the 80° F temperature has been obtained, put the bowl back onto the simmering saucepan and reheat it to a final 88 or 89 degrees.

The chocolate has now been properly tempered! You are now ready to dip whatever confection you choose. To maintain the final temperature as you dip, rather than putting the bowl back over the saucepan and steam, try wrapping an electric heating pad in plastic and setting its temperature on low. Place the bowl of tempered chocolate on the heating pad. This should keep the temperature of your dipping chocolate right where you want it to be. Stir the tempered chocolate often so that it maintains a uniform temperature throughout.

…a quick word about dipping in chocolate...

You can dip anything your heart desires- from shortbread cookies to gummy bears. Find recipes to create your own hard fillings (such as candy caramel). Decorate dipped items by using a piping bag or filling a plastic sandwich bag with melted chocolate and cutting a small hole into one corner. You can then do decorative drizzles.

When dipping fruit, remember that chocolate and water don't mix- thoroughly dry such items as pineapple wedges or apple slices with a paper towel before dipping. Melted milk chocolate chips (just melted, not tempered) are actually ideal for dipping fruit- simply place the dipped fruit onto waxed paper and refrigerate it immediately after dipping it.

White, Milk, And Dark

Cocoa
Just for the record, cocoa is a misspelling of the word cacao that
appeared on a ship's manifest in the 18th century and led to the
replacement of the original word with the now commonly used one....

Chocolate Liquor (Cocoa Mass)
The kernel (nib) of the cocoa bean is ground into a thick paste- a solid
mass that contains no alcohol, called liquor. The liquor is the pure
ground product of the roasted cacao beans, the base for (and main
ingredient) in all chocolate.

Cocoa Butter
Cocoa butter is the vegetable fat from the cacao bean that is extracted
from the chocolate liquor (cocoa mass) when the mass is subjected to
extreme pressure and pressed. Liquid when extracted and solid at room
temperature, it is the main ingredient in white chocolate. It is also
widely used in cosmetics and pharmaceuticals.

Cocoa Powder
Cocoa powder is obtained from the solid (press) cake left after the
cocoa butter is pressed out of the cocoa mass. When ground, two types
of powder are made- natural and Dutch. Natural cocoa powder is pure
and unadulterated, used mostly for baking. Dutch processed cocoa
powder is alkalized to remove its acidity and make it neutral. Dutch
cocoa is milder tasting and blends better with milk.

Unsweetened Chocolate
Unsweetened Chocolate (also known as baking chocolate) is simply
the solid form of cooled chocolate liquor (cocoa mass).

Dark Chocolate

Dark chocolate is really a bit of a misnomer, which is to say that the name is used to describe three relatively similar products, these being sweet, semi-sweet, and bittersweet. The name attached to the chocolate depends on how much sugar is added to the chocolate liquor (cocoa mass). They are all eating chocolates and all are geared toward personal taste.

: Dark chocolate- cocoa liquor(mass), cocoa butter, sugar, vanilla and lecithin.

Milk Chocolate

Milk chocolate is made with the same ingredients as dark chocolate with the addition of milk solids to soften the color and smooth the taste of the chocolate.

: Milk chocolate- cocoa liquor(mass), cocoa butter, sugar, vanilla, lecithin and the addition of milk or milk powder.

White Chocolate

White chocolate is a bit of a misleading term. Made with cocoa butter, milk, sugar and vanilla, it contains no chocolate liquor at all. When buying white chocolate, be wary. Read the label. Some products on the market call themselves white chocolate, but are made with vegetable oil, and contain no cocoa butter at all.

: White chocolate- cocoa butter, sugar, vanilla, lecithin, and milk or milk powder.

What's The Use?

Shampoo and conditioner, bath scents and massage oils, perfumes and cologne, moisturizers and lip balm. Soap and scented candles, incense and air freshener. Chocolate sculptures and chocolate fountains, chocolate sea salt and chocolate vinegar. Molded or marinated, powdered or shaved, bitter, savory or sweet. It is used to treat burns, cough, pregnancy cramps, and headaches. It is thought to strengthen the immune system, fight depression and lower cholesterol.

From the Chocolate Hills in the Philippines, to the Chocolate Mountains of Arizona in America, the entire world is ensconced in chocolate. "The entire world?" You might ask. The simple answer- a resounding yes! Every year on September 13th, the entire planet celebrates International Chocolate Day. If for some reason you didn't know this, mark your calendar and join in the festivities.

Although the origin of International Chocolate Day remains unclear many believe the date was chosen because Milton Hershey, the founder of Hershey's chocolates, was born on September 13th, 1857. This is really neither here nor there. Whatever the origin, the sweet fact is that people all over the world unite every September 13th, from the highlands to the lowlands, from the main lands to the islands and everywhere in between to celebrate chocolate.

For some people, celebrating chocolate is a personal daily ritual, whether consumed in liquid form or eaten. Daily rituals are things taken for granted and done without forethought, like stopping at your favorite coffee shop for a café mocha or fast food outlet for a chocolate shake. Swinging into the convenience store for a bar of chocolate or a bag of candy. For others it has become a tradition to be enjoyed with friends or family during celebrations or holidays. The chocolate bunny on Easter Sunday and the Valentine's Day chocolate filled heart come to mind. Or the wedding that commemorates days to come of great sweetness and days of bitter sorrow with sweet wine and bitter chocolate. Chocolate ritual and tradition has sweetly and subtly crept into our very being and we never even realized it.

Why the tradition?

A daily chocolate habit or ritual is understandable. Chocolate is comfort food. It also contains small amounts of caffeine, which can trigger our endorphins. Simply stated its feel good food. Feelings of comfort and wellbeing can be directly related to traditions. Traditions are handed down not just from peoples of one culture or country one to another, but from family to family. There is a very social aspect tied to the inclusion of chocolate in tradition. Not only personal feelings but sometimes religious aspects are involved.

Holiday Traditions

The two main holidays that embrace chocolate tradition are Christmas and Easter while the most popular day by far for chocolate giving and receiving is Valentine's Day. No surprise there. Gifts of chocolate molded into different shapes have become traditional on all of these holidays.

Valentines Day is no doubt for the adults. Chocolate, considered to be a natural aphrodisiac, plays the starring role. To a kid, Valentines Day holds no romance, it's simply all about the chocolate itself. Ask a kid about love and all you will get is an emphatic "Yuck." What kids do love is Christmas. Easter, along with its chocolate eggs and bunnies is probably a close second. Let's face the facts- Christmas and Easter chocolates were created by grownups for children, although adults also embrace them whole heartedly. A welcoming bowl of foil wrapped mini Christmas trees or Easter eggs is hard to resist. That said, there's nothing quite like watching and wondering what part of a chocolate Santa or Easter bunny a child will eat first. What's the meaning behind eating the head or ears first? Is there unknown malice lurking within?

All over the world, many towns large and small celebrate a Christmas Festival of Lights with beliefs rooted in the Christian faith. The Jewish Festival of Lights known as Hanukkah is also celebrated around the same time frame. No matter what your faith, the festivals of Christmas and Hanukkah revolve around the same things- family, food, and giving thanks.

Christmas
....leave a plate of chocolate chip cookies where Santa can find them. Oh, and maybe some hot cocoa in case he's cold. Chocolate kisses for the reindeer. It's Christmas Eve and the little ones are almost ready for visions of sugar plums. Today, they opened the final door on their advent calendar and gobbled up the last chocolate goody remaining inside. For many children around the world, one of the

biggest sources of excitement during the holiday season is the advent calendar. The cardboard calendar has 24 little perforated doors behind each of which is a piece of chocolate. The premise is to open the first door of the calendar on December 1st and count

down the days until Christmas, ending on December 24th, Christmas Eve.

The first printed Advent Calendar was produced in Germany by Gerhard Lang, in 1908. It was fabricated out of cardboard onto which 24 pictures were affixed. Several years later 24 doors were added behind which were pictures, poems or inspirational verses. The calendars grew in popularity until cardboard was rationed during the Second World War. After the war ended, the tradition was reintroduced in 1946. The first Calendar filled with chocolate became available in 1958.

There is evidence that the infamous Santa made from molded chocolate found his roots in Germany as well. Although Christmas is celebrated throughout the world on December 25th, in Deutschland December 6 is known as St. Nicholas day. On the evening of December 5th, (St. Nicholas Eve) children leave their shoes outside their doors for Father Christmas to fill with goodies. They also leave him small presents of cookies and baked "Weckmann" or bread men, in the shape of St. Nicholas.

The following morning on December 6th- Nikolaustag (St. Nicholas day) the children receive a molded chocolate Santa and a toy. The tradition of seeing the now famous chocolate shaped candy- man (whether in miniature or larger) at Christmas time continues.

Hanukkah

....spin the dreidel and win a pot of chocolate gelt. A dreidel is a four-sided spinning top with a Hebrew letter on each side. It is used during Hanukkah to play a popular children's game that involves spinning the top and betting on which Hebrew letter will be showing when the dreidel stops spinning. Children usually play for a pot of gelt, which are chocolate coins covered in gold colored tin foil. The delicious coins have become a Hanukkah tradition. Gelt literally refers to money as well as to the chocolate coins given to children on the festival of Hanukkah. The custom found its origin in the seventeenth-century when parents gave money to their children for distribution to their teachers. In time, as children demanded their due, money was also given to the youngsters to keep for themselves. An allowance, if you will. This in turn became chocolate money known as gelt (chocolate coins).

The Jewish holiday is celebrated for eight days and nights. Children receive gifts for Hanukkah- often one gift for each of the eight nights of the holiday. The Jewish Festival of Lights also centers on very specific foods, including a delicious dessert known as babka. Think of it as a cousin of the coffee cake. The sweet, swirly loaf, which has roots in Eastern Europe, is traditionally made with chocolate, cinnamon, or both. My vote is on the pure chocolate version.

Easter

The tradition of a door to door chocolate egg delivery service by a rabbit was conceived in Germany sometime in the early17th century. The custom involved children placing straw nests outside the home so that der Osterhase (hare) could deposit brightly colored eggs for them to look for on Easter morning. German and Dutch settlers later brought the ritual of der Osterhase to the U.S. when they settled in Pennsylvania.

Eventually, the tradition caught on and decorative baskets replaced the straw nests, while chocolate eggs and bunnies replaced the previous hard boiled eggs. These days, kids find their goodies inside the house, and later go on a hunt outside. Oh, don't forget to leave the Easter bunny a carrot- a real (not a chocolate) one.

The first chocolate Easter eggs were simply wrapped in decorative paper- evolving into the popular brightly foil encased variety found today in the traditional Easter basket. They were made in Europe in the early 1800's with France and Germany being the forerunners in this new artistic confectionery. Most of the earliest eggs were made of solid chocolate as a hollow egg had to be pressed together by hand with chocolate paste to hold it together.

In 1847 the British chocolate company J.S. Fry and Sons developed a way of combining cocoa butter, cocoa powder and sugar into a paste which could be placed into a mold to produce uniform hollow shaped chocolates that could be individually wrapped. Both solid and hollow eggs could now be mass produced. The earliest chocolate eggs were  made of dark chocolate with a plain smooth surface. Decorated eggs were plain shells enhanced by chocolate piping and marzipan flowers.

The British firm Cadbury Brothers, or specifically Richard Cadbury with his broad artistic flair, played an important part in the development of the chocolate Easter egg mania. Aided with his decorative skills, by 1893 there were no less than 19 different lines on the Cadbury Brothers Easter chocolate list. Most of Richard Cadbury's designs were based on French, Dutch and German originals adapted to Victorian tastes. Many believe he was the pioneer of the decorated chocolate Easter egg industry. In 1923 the company released its first filled eggs and in 1971 the ground breaking Cadbury Creme Eggs appeared.

Valentine's Day

No record exists of romantic celebrations being connected to Valentine's Day prior to a poem by the English poet Geoffrey Chaucer, written in 1382 and known as "The Parliament of Fowls". In the poem he has the birds choosing their mates at the time of year that happens to fall on St. Valentine's Day. He may have unwittingly invented the holiday we know today, as other writers of the time related to his work- comparing the birds' process of wooing a mate to human romantic love.

Early Valentine's Day gifts were simple love letters, and later romantic love notes- written on scented paper in the finest calligraphy a suitor could muster. By the 1600's, tokens of affection started to appear such as gloves, handkerchiefs, and small floral bouquets. Love notes were still very popular (and still are) as gifts on Valentine's Day. The earliest confections (sweets for my sweet) were made out of sugar paste that was dyed and molded then imprinted with a suitable inscription. Known as conversational lozenges, they were all the fashion- especially for anybody who was shy and lacked quality penmanship. It didn't take long for the gents to realize that chocolate was an even sweeter way to a lady's heart.

In 1800's England, the Cadbury Brothers were enjoying the immense popularity that came along with making and perfecting eating chocolate. George was in charge of production, his brother Richard in charge of marketing. Always artistic, Richard designed beautifully decorated boxes that helped to enhance the chocolates appeal. In 1861, in a genius marketing move, Richard Cadbury created the first ever heart shaped box for Valentine's Day. The chocolate filled heart shaped box was an immediate success, is until this day, and always will be.

Love, Chocolate, and the Heart Shaped Box

 The Aztec ruler Montezuma believed that chocolate was an aphrodisiac and routinely drank it before entering his harem, greatly increasing the association of chocolate with love and romance. It seems he was ahead of his time. Modern day science suggests that

phenylethylamine, a chemical found in chocolate, can lead to feelings of pleasure and attraction. This Valentine's Day, after a romantic dinner, skip the vanilla torte and go straight for the chocolate mousse. It is light and airy, the perfect complement to your choice of any of the mixed chocolates inside your true loves heart shaped box. Oh, and a cup of gourmet coffee or a demitasse of espresso to enhance the experience couldn't hurt either. Chocolate and coffee- now that's what I call the perfect marriage.

The Perfect Marriage

A decadent calorie filled slice of chocolate cake, paired with a rich steaming cup of gourmet Arabica coffee. A dark chocolate hot cocoa paired with the coffee laced lady fingers in a slice of tiramisu. Iced coffee and double chocolate cookies. Surely you can relate. Coffee and  chocolate are the perfect union. Chocolate 'marries' with coffee. The flavors of the two make for the perfect pair. Try a scoop of chocolate ice cream topped with a double shot of espresso and the concept will be driven home.

There are many similarities between the cacao bean and the coffee bean which at this point may or may not surprise you. The thing that I find most fascinating is that coffee originated in Africa and was transported to South America, where Brazil now produces the most coffee, while chocolate originated in South America and was transported to Africa, where the Ivory Coast now produces the most chocolate. Crazy.

Dates to Remember

September 13th
International Chocolate Day.

September 29th
International Coffee Day.

The earliest explorers plying the trade winds filled their holds with coffee and cacao understanding the significance of their newfound treasures.

Two Beans

: Both coffee and chocolate are derived from a fruit- the seeds (beans) of the coffee cherry and the seeds (beans) of the cacao pod.

: Both fruits are hand selected, that is to say they are picked or harvested only by hand, and only when they have reached the optimum stage of ripeness.

: Early findings reveal that the pulpy mucilage of both the coffee cherry and the cacao pod were used to ferment into a beverage that contained alcohol.

: Both beans contain the chemicals caffeine and theobromine which are mild stimulants. Coffee contains more caffeine, chocolate more theobromine.

: In ancient times, cacao and coffee beans were both used for religious purposes. In Central America, Mayan priests would mix cacao with blood to sprinkle on crops to ensure a good harvest, while in Africa the monks who inhabited the monasteries imbibed coffee to give them energy and also to keep them alert during prayer.

: Kings and tribal leaders understood the importance of energized troops. In wartime, the early African warriors consumed coffee mixed with fat to sustain them, while Central American Aztec warriors mixed dried powdered cacao with corn and water for sustenance.

: The Mayans poured their drinking chocolate from cup to cup to obtain froth considering it to be the soul of the drink. The Turks boiled their coffee to obtain froth- pouring it into their cups before the liquid as they considered the froth to be the best part of the cup.

: As times became more civilized, circa 1650, in London, England, you could choose whether to enjoy a stimulating beverage in either a coffee shop or a chocolate house. Both were known as political hot beds, and in those days were patronized mainly by men.

: In the 1700's, the Swedish botanist Carl Linnaeus named both coffee and chocolate. Coffea Arabica, also known as the coffee shrub of Arabia, is believed to be the first species of coffee ever to be cultivated. Theobroma Cacao when translated from Latin literally means food of the gods. Linnaeus classified and named nearly eight thousand plants.

: Both coffee and chocolate were part of a soldiers rations during the World Wars. A cup of courage and a bar of bravery. A comforting piece of home when you were far afield.

: Both chocolate and coffee have blasted off and departed from the earth's atmosphere and traveled into outer space.

: Both are grown in regions close to the equator. The equator is an imaginary band that stretches around the middle of the world and encircles the entire globe. Cacao trees flourish between 20 degrees N. and 20 degrees S. of the equator (the twenty- twenty zone), while coffee is bounded by the Tropics of Capricorn and Cancer.

: When referring to chocolate the imaginary band is known as the Cocoa Belt, when referring to coffee it is known as the Bean Belt. Since the equatorial line encircles the entire planet, Hawaii falls into this category. Hawaii grows both coffee and chocolate.

: Since both are grown in regions close to the equator, they thrive in the temperate equatorial climate where the humidity is high, and the temperatures are between 65 and 85 degrees yearlong with optimum rainfall between 60- 80 inches per year.

: They are both grown on plants that mature into large trees which are pruned to a suitable height for harvesting purposes. The two most popular strains of coffee are Arabica (the best) and Robusta. The two most popular strains of cacao are Criollo (the best) and Forastero.

: Arabica coffee beans account for 75-80 percent of the world's yearly production of coffee and is the basis for all gourmet coffees sold. Forastero cacao beans account for 75-80 percent of the world's yearly production of cacao and is the basis for almost all chocolate sold.

: Chocolate connoisseurs are buying more and more Fair Trade and single origin chocolates such as Criollo, while Fair Trade coffees and single origin Organic Arabicas enjoy notoriety.

: Both plants produce beans which are harvested by hand for the best quality, and go through very similar processes to obtain the best end result. Once harvested, the beans both have to be extracted from the sweet mucilage inside the fruit that surrounds them- coffee from the cherry, cacao from the pod.

: Once extracted, they both need to be fermented. Once fermented, they need to be dried. Once dried, they need to be stored. Once stored, they need to be shipped. Once shipped, they need to be roasted. Once roasted, they need to be ground.

: The final grinding and roasting of both coffee and chocolate are crucial elements to a quality end product. All of the work done previously by thousands of people - seeding, planting, maintaining, harvesting, processing, and shipping come down to one thing and one thing alone- a single dried bean. Be it coffee or cocoa, what happens to that bean is the responsibility of the chocolatiers and artisanal roasters. Or in better terms a craftsperson. As long as the beans have been handled properly beforehand, the roast level is the single most important component of the flavor achieved in the final product. This is true whether in a large factory or in a privately owned cafe or boutique.

As the world becomes commercialized, people tend to visit the big box stores to shop for mainstream products, although there has always been a niche for entrepreneurial spirit. Gourmet coffee by the cup has risen in popularity to the point of being sold in gas stations. You can now buy bulk Arabica coffee beans at your local grocery store.

Gourmet chocolate has been around a long time as well. Artisans sell chocolate by country of origin, such as Ecuador and Madagascar. Single origin just means that all of the chocolate contained in the confection comes from the same place. In a perfect world, you could order a cup of Mexican Chiapas coffee with a piece of Mexican Chiapas chocolate cake. That day may well come.

Take some time for yourself and forgo the mainstream once in a while. Visit a chocolate artisan and sample their confections. Buy Arabica coffee and grind it yourself. And on a daily basis, from your morning coffee until your bedtime hot cocoa, never take for granted the Coffee Cherry and the Cocoa Pod. Coffee and cacao. Go ahead.Embrace your addiction.

www.ingramcontent.com/pod-product-compliance
Lightning Source LLC
Chambersburg PA
CBHW070159290526
45789CB00002B/832